Muhammad

Muhammad

The Story of a Prophet and Reformer

Sarah Conover

Decoration by Iman K. Hasan

Skinner House Books

Boston

www.skinnerhouse.org

Printed in the United States

Cover and text design by Suzanne Morgan
Front cover photo: dome ceiling at imam mosque in Isfahan, Iran.
Copyright © 2012, Abby V. Anderson

print ISBN: 978-1-55896-704-5
eBook ISBN: 978-1-55896-705-2

6 5 4 3 2 1
15 14 13

Library of Congress Cataloging-in-Publication Data
Conover, Sarah.
  Muhammad: the story of a prophet and reformer / by Sarah Conover.
    p. cm.
   ISBN 978-1-55896-704-5 (pbk. : alk. paper)—ISBN 978-1-55896-705-2
(ebook) 1. Muhammad, Prophet, d. 632—Biography. I. Title.
  BP75.C65 2013
  297.6'3—dc23
  [B]
                              2012048412

Excerpts from the Royal Aal al-Bayt Institute's translation of the Quran reprinted by permission of the Royal Islamic Strategic Studies Centre.

For my dear Muslim friends and friends-to-be
who demonstrate with love and generosity
the blessings of their faith

—S. C.

Contents

Acknowledgments

First and foremost, even though it cost me a summer of exacting revisions, I'd like to thank Dr. Freda Shamma, from the Foundation for the Advancement and Development of Education and Learning (FADEL), for her tireless attention to detail. The book is much the better for her guidance over the two years of its creation. Thank you to Elizabeth Deubler, Richard Smith, and Nathan Robnett-Conover for their feedback on the early drafts. Much gratitude to Mary Benard at Skinner House Books for allowing me to veer from our original idea of a small book for children to a much longer work for a multigenerational audience because I felt so strongly that the fuller story needed telling. Thank you also to Ms. Benard for soliciting the feedback of a distinguished line-up of experts so that the details of Muhammad's life are presented as accurately as possible. To that effect, I am grateful most especially for the time and consideration of Dr. Ahmed Ragab, Richard T. Watson

Assistant Professor of Science and Religion at Harvard Divinity School. Thanks also to Anne El-Moslimany, Founding Director of the Islamic School of Seattle, and to Dr. Ali Asani, Director of the Prince Alwaleed bin Talal Islamic Studies Program at Harvard University. I'd like to acknowledge with gratitude Abdelmajid Fouad, who provided phonemic transcription of Arabic names and phrases into the Latin alphabet. Finally, my boundless appreciation to my husband, Doug Robnett, for believing in the importance of this project to build bridges of understanding between Muslims and non-Muslims. His unreserved support of my work at home and during our travels through Islamic cultures cannot be overstated.

Foreword

As I read this book, I kept thinking of one of my favorite lines in Islam: "God is beautiful and loves beauty." The book you hold contains a beautiful story beautifully told. I wish this were the case more often, but the truth is that the tale too often told about the Prophet Muhammad (peace be upon him) in our times is twisted to the point of deformation—which just makes *Muhammad: The Story of a Prophet and Reformer* that much more meaningful and powerful.

I was told the target audience of this book is young people, and so I started reading it with two sets of eyes: the eyes of a Muslim father who is constantly on the lookout for material that will give my young boys a deeper understanding of their faith and the eyes of an interfaith leader whose organization, Interfaith Youth Core, focuses on inspiring young people to bridge the faith divide. Both sets of eyes found much to love and admire here. I especially appreciated the way the author brought to life the key role that non-Muslims played in the life and Prophethood of Muhammad. How two Christians, Bahirah and Waraqah, were among the first to recognize Muhammad's spiritual significance. And how a pagan, Muhammad's uncle Abu Talib, risked his own life to protect the Prophet from those who wished him harm. So frequently we hear the perversion that Islam is a tradition that seeks either separation from others or domination over them. These stories highlight the relational dimensions of Islam, an important lesson for both Muslims and non-Muslims.

Which brings me to my next point: Even though I started reading this book with the eyes of a father and interfaith activist, I found myself enjoying it, and learning a great deal, as a writer and teacher on Islam. This is to say that, like the best books meant for young adults, there is much here for those who are older and fancy themselves wiser. I personally found the description of Muhammad's private life with his wife Khadija and their daughters especially moving.

It occurred to me about halfway through this book that it felt a bit short to be a full biography of Muhammad. After reading how the author told the tale of the initial revelations, the early days of the Prophet's preaching, the unconditional love and support his wife Khadija displayed, the generosity with which Muhammad engaged his detractors, I was eager to read about the episodes in the Prophet's later life. Alas, the book ends in 622, the year the Prophet makes the Hijrah from Mecca to Medina, about halfway through his Prophetic mission. I confess to letting out a deep sad sigh when I realized that I would not get the author's take on those final ten years in this book. Part of me wished the publisher had demanded the whole biography. But I suppose there is no higher compliment for a reader to pay a writer than to say, "I wish the book were longer."

—Eboo Patel
Founder and President, Interfaith Youth Core
April 13, 2013

The Orphan

Aminah awoke early, swung her legs onto the dirt floor and paused. Muhammad, her infant son, lay fast asleep on their mat of woven palms. She reached over and laid a gentle hand on his chest, reassuring herself of his steady breath. The intuition that he would be a great leader had come to Aminah in a vision. She also noticed curious signs throughout her pregnancy. Remembering these, she rose and entered the dim courtyard where her servant, Barakah, lit a small fire of camel dung.

"*Umti sabahan*, good morning!" Barakah said. Aminah returned the greeting with a smile and watched as Barakah poured some water in a pot for tea and placed it over the fire. Still sleep-filled, gazing at the small curls of steam beginning to rise from the water, Aminah soon lost herself in worry. She frowned. Muhammad's father had died and the boy's life was bound to be a struggle. He had inherited only five camels and a small flock of sheep and goats. His father had been a member of the proud Banu Hashim clan, but a fatherless child in sixth-century Arabia lacked his most important protector.

The softly approaching light and the clang and clamor of men setting up their stalls in the marketplace startled Aminah out of her concerns. Barakah readied some bread, dabbing each slice with a little yoghurt, then cut some dates in half and mounded them on a small plate. Placing the food and steeping tea on a tray on the floor, she quietly left the room to complete other chores. Aminah lowered herself onto one of the cushions lining the wall, moved the tray close, and ate.

Dust, already hanging thick in Mecca's air, meant that various tribes from all over the northwest had come to trade at the bazaar today. Mecca was simply sand and mud-bricked buildings. Without a blade of green, the city had to rely on distant farms for all its food. Dates came from Yathrib in the north; Syria, further north, sent barley; and in some seasons, fresh fruit and vegetables arrived from Yemen. Although the tribes of Arabia came to honor their gods at Mecca's sacred shrine, the Kaaba, they also counted on doing good business. Mecca was one of the few cities in the vast desert where caravans and merchants came to trade.

When Aminah finished her meal, she looked in on Muhammad; he was awake but quiet—wide-eyed and listening to the commotion from the bazaar. She, as well as others, appreciated this calm quality: His aunts chided that, no matter what storms roiled about him, Muhammad seemed untroubled. She wiped the circles of fresh dust from his nostrils and face.

Aminah resolved that today she'd find a Bedouin wet nurse to raise the boy in the fresh air of the desert. Many families had only recently left the freedom of roaming the desert to settle in Mecca. Like them, Aminah believed the city too polluted for raising a healthy child. It was too full of strangers and their strange customs. The Bedouins, however—the tribes that bred sheep and camels in the desert wilderness—could introduce Muhammad to the old ways. They could show him the strength of the nomadic life. She hoped that the Bedouin women looking for nurslings had already made their way to Mecca this morning. She must talk with them.

Aminah bundled Muhammad in a thin camelhair blanket and donned her finest robe and headscarf. The fact that her boy had no father would signal to the Bedouins that he had little wealth for their wages, but she prayed a couple might find it in their hearts to take her fatherless child.

She wove through the crowd, ignoring until later the stalls brimming with goods. On her left, she passed an elderly Jewish man who sat with his eyes closed, murmuring prayers; next to him, his sons sold fresh dates from their orchards in Yathrib. Oh to have some! She extended a hand to test their plumpness but pulled back, remembering her single task today: Muhammad's future.

Not far off, the silhouettes of Bedouin camels stood against the horizon. The nomads knew to keep their distance from the diseases and turmoil of city life. Aminah quickened her pace in their direction.

The Shepherd

This morning, like every morning of his desert life with the Bedouins, Muhammad sprang to his feet and shook off the night as well as his blanket. He loved to get up before the sun. He never knew if the sound that woke him was an owl snatching a last meal or the soft bells of the animals grazing, but dawn was too exciting a time to sleep. He had only a month left before he rejoined his mother in Mecca.

Because he was an orphan, only the poorest couple had offered to take Muhammad seven years ago—they owned but a few sheep and a single camel. "It was a terrible drought," his Bedouin mother, Halimah, told Muhammad about the year he came to their family. "We had nothing. I traveled to Mecca on my grey donkey, and we had with us an old camel that could not produce one drop of milk. Our son kept us awake all night wailing from hunger, for I had nothing to feed him." Since the time Muhammad joined them, however, the animals' udders overflowed with milk and no one went hungry. His presence seemed a blessing from God, from Allah.

Muhammad swept aside the tent flap of camel hide and ran to the small campfire. Halimah, anticipating his early appearance, handed him a large cup of camel-milk yoghurt. Muhammad smiled at her and gulped down his breakfast. Before he followed the older boys to the herds, Halimah pushed a cloth-bound parcel of dates into his hands—lunch.

By the time Muhammad reached a small incline where the sheep grazed, the sky flushed full with morning. A slice of sun hit the rock he stood upon, and the air was so clear that the voices of Bedouin families far below sounded as if they came from right beside him. Everyone was awake by now to enjoy the coolest part of the day. Muhammad joined the other young herders who stood in a clump chatting while keeping an eye on their camels and sheep. As the sun crested the horizon however, all the boys looked up and hushed. It seemed like the birds, too, paused in their singing, spellbound by the spark of a new day.

The hours unfolded and the heat soared uncomfortably, but Muhammad paid close attention and brought the shepherds new questions every day. How does the sound of a sheep's cry change from one of hunger to one of danger? How do you train a camel to kneel on command? How often do goats and sheep need water? How long can a camel really go without it? The Bedouin boys were happy to teach

Muhammad their special knowledge, the knowledge of desert survival passed on by their fathers and forefathers.

After lunch, Muhammad found a place to rest in the shade with a sweeping view of the flocks. Unlike most others, he didn't need constant company; often, he felt content to listen to the wilderness and simply watch. He knelt down and fingered a tiny green shoot that caught his eye. It grew out of a crack in a rock! No matter what he learned in the city of Mecca, no matter if he was an orphan—a nobody—he hoped always to notice these simple signs of creation, these everyday miracles. God had much to teach through nature. Muhammad would miss his desert days, but he felt certain he'd return to its peacefulness many times in the future.

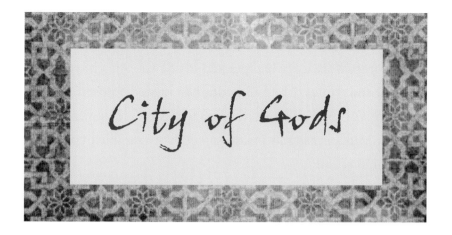

City of Gods

"It *is* true!" the Meccan girl whispered to her friend. "The Kaaba was built by the Prophet Abraham and his son, Ishmael. That's what our forefathers tell us, and that's what the Jews and Christians say, too!"

"Well," said her friend, "Uncle says it was built by Adam, the very first man." Sliding along a nearby wall, both girls inched closer to the Kaaba, but soon stopped. In a wide circle some distance from the Kaaba, 360 statues of tribal gods surrounded the building. Inside the Kaaba there were more, as well as a painting of the Virgin Mary and the Christ child.

"But why can't *we* go in?" asked her friend.

The young girl gripped her friend's hand. "No! It's only for grownups. Some terrible misfortune may happen to your family if you insult one of their gods. See how all the men touch the statues outside for a blessing and then bring them gifts inside the Kaaba?" She nodded toward the solemn travelers entering the building.

Listening to the girls, Muhammad smiled a little, having heard this same conversation a dozen times since his return to Mecca. He had peeked inside the ancient building a few times while Grandfather busied himself with visitors to the Kaaba, visitors known as religious pilgrims. What Muhammad saw inside looked like a jumble of paintings and statues.

Muhammad turned toward his grandfather, Abd al-Muttalib, who provided water to the pilgrims from all over Arabia. Not so long ago, he had rediscovered the Spring of Zamzam—the reason the Kaaba had been built in this very spot. For centuries, the well was lost beneath the sand, probably buried by marauders. Yet a dream came to Muhammad's grandfather over and over, telling him where to look for the well. Finally, he took a pickaxe to the spot and dug until he hit the hidden well's lid. Since then, Abd al-Muttalib held the authority of dispensing the water.

Muhammad bounded over to where Grandfather stationed himself at the Iraq corner, the northwest corner of the Kaaba. Preferring shade, Abd al-Muttalib set up a pallet on the ground and greeted travelers, pilgrims, and the men of Mecca. Since he was the chief of the Quraysh tribe, no one was allowed to share the spot with him—no one, that is, except his beloved grandson, Muhammad, who was ever at his side. Grandfather had even given the boy his name, Muhammad, meaning praiseworthy. He often told one and all, "Leave him be, for by God, a great future is his." So much did Abd al-Muttalib believe in his grandson's future that he even brought him to the assemblies of Meccan chiefs. Rarely did the eighty-year-old grandfather hesitate to ask the seven-year-old Muhammad's opinion, even on important matters.

Today there were many visitors, but Muhammad heard his grandfather's hearty voice and laugh above the noise. He found Abd al-Muttalib speaking with a tall stranger. Eyeing the pilgrim—his turban and robes shimmering with elaborate silk stitching and embroidery—Muhammad knew the pilgrim to be very wealthy and from very far away. Grandfather pointed the man in the direction of the well to fill his camel skin.

Because Muhammad never tired of hearing the bucket drop into the well's mouth and splash the water deep in its belly below, Grandfather sometimes allowed him to help the servants. With a silent nod and smile from Abd al-Muttalib, Muhammad knew he had permission today. Running ahead of this latest visitor, he waited beside the well where the servants made room for him to grab the rope and lower the bucket. Since Muhammad was still too small to haul it up alone, the servants helped him pull the vessel to the top without a drop spilled. Then as the man held his camel skin steady, Muhammad filled its narrow opening with cool water. Slinging the skin back over his shoulder, the pilgrim gave Muhammad a wide smile.

Returning to the Kaaba's entrance, Muhammad looked at the long line of pilgrims in front of the sacred building, each with a god to worship. He stood and watched. There were so many gods in there, so many different names and rules for each. Did people believe all these gods could be kept happy? How could statues made by men have any power over men? It made no sense.

Just then, he felt the comforting strength of Grandfather's arm across his shoulders. Abd al-Muttalib was talking in a hushed voice to a traveler. "Just a child and he has lost not only his father, but now, last month, his mother too," said Grandfather.

Muhammad stared at the ground, overcome with sadness. Since his mother's death, grief often shadowed him. Muhammad felt the stranger's eyes upon him as Grandfather continued, "His mother, Aminah, went to visit her husband's grave in Yathrib with my grandson, but she grew ill during the return journey and passed away before reaching home." He tucked Muhammad in closer. "It was so sudden! We miss her so!" Grandfather seemed to run out of words. The visitor nodded thoughtfully. Muhammad did not look up, even though it seemed impolite. After a while, the pilgrim placed a hand softly on the boy's head and then walked away. *At least I have a grandfather*, Muhammad told himself. *At least a grandfather*.

Signs

Muhammad stretched his arm out in front of him and measured how many hand-widths between sun and horizon: five hands—five hours—before sunset. He turned to his uncle, Abu Talib, with the information. Muhammad was twelve and determined to be helpful on his first merchant caravan.

"*Halummu*—let's go!" shouted Abu Talib, spurring his camel forward toward Bostra, the evening stop for rest and water. Muhammad returned his uncle's good cheer with a smile and then twisted around to watch the caravan's thirty or so riders behind him. A family's wealth was measured in the number of camels owned, and each of the men had a half-dozen loaded with goods to trade. In this harsh country, camels provided transportation, their meat and milk served as food, and their hides supplied waterskins and warmth. Muhammad delighted in seeing the prized animals trot, the tassels of their colorful harnesses, blankets, and saddles looking like bouncing rainbows.

Some of the men slapped their camels' shoulders with a crop to hasten them onward; others shouted until the camels cantered. The men managed to stay secure and smooth on their saddles by looping one leg around the camel's single hump and locking one ankle under the other ankle. Muhammad had already mastered the skill living among the Bedouins.

When Muhammad's grandfather died not long ago, his uncle, Abu Talib, became his guardian. Abu Talib and his wife, Fatima, had a large family and were poor, but if food was scarce, Muhammad's aunt insisted on feeding him even before her own children—she wanted to be as much of a mother to him as possible.

Muhammad helped his new family by pasturing their sheep and goats in the valleys and hills beyond Mecca. Most days he shepherded alone, but now and then, he accompanied his uncle on small journeys. This trip to Syria, however, was Muhammad's first chance to participate in a full caravan. He had jumped at the chance.

The camels knew they were nearing Bostra before their riders did. Ears tipped forward, nostrils flaring with the first scents of water and trees, they rumbled with excitement. Near Bostra, the monk Bahirah closely watched their approach. He'd seen many caravans come this way before, but never like this: A single cloud seemed to follow the caravan, always placing itself between the sun and one or two of the riders.

Bahirah was a Christian hermit living in a solitary dwelling. He stared at the line of men and camels, not quite believing his eyes. The cloud was one of the signs foretelling a Prophet of the Arab people. He'd learned of it in the manuscripts left by generations of monks before him.

Bahirah ran inside. While his eyes adjusted to the darkness, he used his hands to feel along the surface of a table until he found the ancient books. Gingerly, Bahirah slid out the third manuscript from the top and carried it to his bench outside the small mud-brick cell. Resting it on both knees, he opened the heavy bound parchment, scanning each page until he found what he was looking for: Among the portents, it said that the future Prophet would be shaded from the sun by a cloud; he would be an orphan; his dreams would contain certain symbols, and he would have the mark of Prophethood between his shoulder blades. Could it be, wondered Bahirah, that this special person rode in the caravan?

Gathering all the food he had, Bahirah sent a message to the caravan: "Men of Quraysh, I am preparing a meal for you, and I invite every one of you—young and old—to eat with me."

Soon the men gathered in the shade of an acacia tree near Bahirah's dwelling. They left the youngest among them, Muhammad, in charge of the animals. The monk had laid out small plates of dates, nuts, and raisins for them on a palm mat. Several dripping camel skins of fresh water hung from the tree's branches.

Inviting the merchants to sit down in a circle, Bahirah scrutinized the men, but he did not sense any of the other signs he had hoped for. Yet the cloud was too important a portent to dismiss. At last Bahirah asked, "Men of Quraysh, are there none you have left behind?"

Muhammad's uncle answered, "A boy remains to look after the animals." It was clear from Bahirah's expression that they must fetch Muhammad right away. Apologizing for the mistake, Abu Talib hurried to his nephew and brought him to the monk. They made room for Muhammad to sit next to Bahirah while they passed to him what was left of the meal.

The kind old hermit watched Muhammad closely while he ate and asked him to describe his dreams and various other experiences in his life. Muhammad, respectful of elders, answered politely between bites of food. Soon all of the men quieted, sensing that Bahirah was searching for something important in Muhammad's answers.

After Muhammad took a drink of water, Bahirah asked the boy if he would remove his cloak, so that Bahirah might examine the skin between Muhammad's shoulder blades. He didn't disclose what he saw to the others, but they all saw his eyes widen in astonishment. The boy carried the mark of Prophethood.

Convinced now of Muhammad's great destiny, Bahirah turned to Abu Talib. "What is your relation to the boy?"

Having adopted Muhammad as his own son, he replied,

"He is my son."

The monk shook his head from side to side, the prophecy still fresh in his mind. "No. He cannot be your son. This boy's father cannot be alive."

"Well, in fact," said Abu Talib, "My brother died while the boy was in his mother's womb. Muhammad is his son, not mine."

Bahirah felt that he had closed in on the last sign the ancient scripture predicted. His heart raced. "Yes, that is the truth!" said Bahirah, brightening. He laid one hand over Muhammad's and one hand over Abu Talib's, as if giving them each a blessing. "When you take your brother's son back home," he said to Abu Talib, "guard him well. There are great things in store for him."

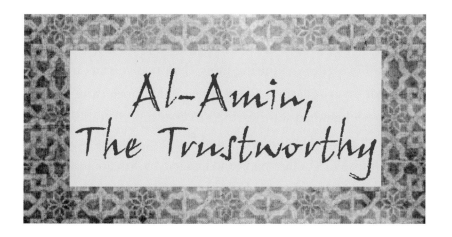

Al-Amin, The Trustworthy

The summer sun scorched the hills surrounding Mecca.
Under the shelter of a desert ghaf tree, Muhammad watched
a beetle scuttle into the shade, its black back shimmering iridescent green. No matter the season, Muhammad's
duty as a shepherd took him outside the city's turmoil. He
appreciated this, even in the searing heat—just as when he
lived with the Bedouins, he found the quiet days allowed
him ample time to think. Like most people of the desert,
he neither read nor wrote, but having heard something even
once, he could put it to memory, word for word. There was
much to contemplate in the peace of God's wilderness.

After the monk Bahirah's warning, Muhammad's uncle
insisted that he stay close to Mecca until he learned the
skills to defend himself. When Abu Talib looked at his
nephew, he saw a young man of medium height, slim but
broad-shouldered. He might not be the strongest of the
Quraysh at swordsmanship like his husky uncle and play-

mate, Hamza, but no one possessed keener eyesight than Muhammad. On their journeys together, Abu Talib remembered his nephew counting more than twelve stars in the Pleiades constellation, a feat none could equal. Abu Talib knew Muhammad was destined to be a superb archer.

After years of shepherding and learning the skills to protect himself, Muhammad, encouraged by his uncle, took up the business of trade. He was asked to join his Quraysh kinsmen on many caravans, and over time, because of his dependability and success, Muhammad found himself in charge of other merchants' goods. Despite his orphan status, Muhammad's reputation began to grow in Mecca and beyond, earning him the nickname al-Amin—the Reliable, the Trustworthy, the Honest.

One of the wealthiest merchants in all of Mecca to hear the rumor of al-Amin was a woman named Khadija. A distant cousin of Muhammad and fifteen years his elder, she was anxious to hire him as her agent to take goods to the north and sell them. Yesterday, she had sent word through a servant, and she expected Muhammad to arrive sometime this morning to discuss her business idea. Khadija surveyed her office. Angling through the eastern window from the courtyard, the sun landed on a small rug in the center of the room, warming its reds to the color of campfire embers. It reminded Khadija of her ties to her Bedouin grandparents. It was not so long ago that many of her tribe left the desert behind to live in this city.

Bending to straighten the pillows resting against the mud walls, Khadija ran a few fingers over their surface, delighted with the ancient symbols worked into the leather. She thought of how proud her first two husbands, both passed away, would be of her visible success in business. Khadija was one of the few—a woman no less—who could afford a rug instead of a palm mat for her home, and who could afford to pay a leather master to ornament her pillows. She had used her inheritance from each of her husbands well.

She wanted to make an impression on the young man. This trip to Syria was costly. Business arrangements were never quick: Many details had to be sorted—how many hides to sell, their quality and size, and how many camels needed to carry them. She'd already decided to pay Muhammad twice the normal fee to make sure he would accept her offer. She would also send along Maysarah, her most trusted servant, to test Muhammad. He would tell her exactly what kind of man al-Amin really was.

The arrangements went smoothly, and Muhammad and Maysarah returned within a month of their departure. In private, Khadija listened carefully to Maysarah's recounting of the journey. He told a strange story of a Christian monk who watched Muhammad resting in the shade of a tree. The monk, named Nestor, asked Maysarah about Muhammad's identity. "I told him he was of the Quraysh tribe. And then the monk told me, 'It is a Prophet that sits beneath the tree.'"

Khadija delighted in Maysarah's telling of the journey. Muhammad's success far exceeded what she'd expected to earn. However, she felt pleased with al-Amin for more than just the business triumph: Khadija began to wonder if he would consider marriage.

As soon as Muhammad left her home, she sent her friend, Nufaysah, to inquire why he did not marry. Nufaysah hurried to Abu Talib's home, where Muhammad rested from his travels. She found him in his uncle's courtyard, keeping his youngest cousins happy in play as he loved to do.

Nufaysah waited until Muhammad directed the children's attention elsewhere, so she could ask him Khadija's question. His answer was simple and plain: "I have no money to marry." He cast his eyes downward, concealing embarrassment. He hadn't inherited anything from his father.

Nufaysah smiled, and continued. "But if you were given the means to marry, and made a union where beauty, property, nobility, and wealth were plentiful, would you not agree to it?"

Looking up, Muhammad asked, "Who is she?"

"Khadija," said the woman.

"But how could such a marriage be mine?" he asked, disbelief on his face.

"Leave that to me!" said Nufaysah, brightening.

"For my part then," said Muhammad, "I am willing."

When Khadija heard this answer, she sent word to Muhammad to visit soon. She had lost two husbands, but from what she had seen of Muhammad, from the kindness and honesty he showed her already, her mind was set.

Khadija's servant led Muhammad to the small apartment off the courtyard where Khadija waited for him. She welcomed him and invited Muhammad to sit on the opposite pallet. Another servant brought them juice. When the servant left, Khadija took a breath, for she was about to do something very unusual for the time—ask a man to marry her. "Son of my uncle," she began, "I love you for your kinship with me, and because you are always fair, never taking sides between people for this or that; I love you for your trustworthiness, for the beauty of your character, and for the truth of your words." And then she proposed.

At the Center of the World

Thieves had easily sprung over the Kaaba's eight-foot walls and stolen treasure from its vault. The news traveled quickly, and by the time the merchants opened their stalls at the bazaar, a large crowd jostled in front of the ancient building, the place most Arabs considered the holy center of the world.

"Who would do such an awful thing?" asked an old woman, wiping tears with her robe.

"Such a tragedy!" lamented the others around her.

"We will find the thieves and they will be punished!" shouted a man who climbed a nearby wall to get a better look.

Already, a tribal council of the four leading clans gathered inside the Kaaba, inspecting the damage and seeing what had vanished. Such a crime must never happen again. Their course of action was quickly decided: The ancient building needed to have higher walls and be covered and secured. A Greek ship had recently run aground on the coast. Its timbers could be salvaged for a sturdy roof, solving a great problem in this treeless land. Perhaps, thought the council, the theft and the shipwreck were all signs from God, Allah, to go ahead.

Work began immediately. First, the men removed the stone that fell from the sky—the sacred Black Stone—from the Kaaba's east corner for safeguarding until it could be put back. Next, they carried away the building's crumbling mud bricks until they reached a foundation of hard green cobblestones. They would reconstruct the Kaaba upon these.

Soon enough, new walls rose higher each day, but so too did long-simmering clan rivalries. In their nomadic tradition, honor, not riches, was life's prize; setting the sacred Black Stone in its place would secure a clan's standing for eternity.

"Our clan alone," one chief claimed, "is the most respected in Mecca, in all of Arabia, and deserves to position the sacred Black Stone."

"No!" cried one of the other leaders. "Ours is the largest, so it makes the most sense for us to place it." The competition continued between the clans, and in four short days, all efforts at cooperation were poisoned. The four clans had each claimed a side of the Kaaba, and worked only on their single wall. The men hissed insults at one another, some under their breath, and some loud enough to trigger blows.

By night, the clans met separately, and secretly, to forge plans for a fight that would end the dispute. By day, the tribal council met, searching for a solution that would not result in bloodshed. Each of the clan leaders had visited cities where laws of the land prevented small conflicts like this from exploding. To the north in Syria, Roman justice ruled; to the south in Abyssinia, a Christian king, the Negus, commanded. Mecca's people only recently traded the freedom of the nomadic life for a settled one. Justice by battle was still their custom.

Several councils later, with the crisis at a pitch and war looming, the oldest man present, Abu Umayyah, proposed a solution. "Oh men of Quraysh," he said, "take a mediator between you to settle this quarrel." Looking at the men's faces, he saw the tension unravel just enough that the chiefs would consider his suggestion. He continued, "Let the first person to enter the gate of the Kaaba tomorrow settle this dispute fairly."

Muhammad, on a business journey during the theft, had returned to Mecca just the day before. An early riser and eager to resume his prayers at the Kaaba, he was the first to enter the next day. He halted at the doorway, seeing the council of men and sensing an angry impasse. The clan chiefs sat far apart, their elders clustered behind them.

All eyes turned to Muhammad, whose appearance caused a stirring of ease in the room. "It is al-Amin, the honest and trustworthy!" said a few men at once, relieved.

While they explained the situation to him, Muhammad listened impartially, letting each chief speak his peace. In a short time, each of the four leaders agreed, "We can accept Muhammad's judgment."

A ray of sun slanting through the window drew Muhammad's attention. Fine specs of dust hovered in a single shaft of light. He wondered, what could hold the four factions together? After brief thought, Muhammad suggested a solution so obvious and fair it startled everyone. "Bring me a cloak," he said. When they brought it, he laid it on the ground, and straightened all the edges so it was perfectly square. He then asked for the sacred Black Stone, and placed it in the exact center of the cloak. The room hushed. "Let each clan take hold of a border of the cloak." The men rose from their cushions and, clan by clan, grasped the cloak's edge.

Muhammad then said, "Lift the cloak up, everyone at the same time." They did. Holding it so the stone did not move, the men carefully followed Muhammad to the Kaaba's east corner where a space in the bricks waited for the Black Stone. Muhammad then reached to the center of the cloak, lifted the stone, and placed it exactly where it had been for centuries.

Home

"*Abana* is here!" shouted Zaynab, who saw Muhammad first. The three sisters—Zaynab, Ruqayyah, and Umm Kulthum—ran to greet him. Zaynab, the oldest, herded the younger ones together to welcome their father, who had returned from a few days in the mountains east of Mecca. Once a year, Muhammad dedicated a number of days during the month called Ramadan to quiet reflection. When Muhammad's food and water ran out, sometimes he came home to resupply and take care of the family business. At other times, Khadija, not wanting his prayers interrupted, brought food to him or they would meet halfway.

Umm Kulthum, the youngest but for the new infant, trembled with eagerness when her father entered the courtyard. Her older sisters kept her in check. Muhammad kneeled down and opened his arms wide. The girls rushed over and leapt into them, each talking over the other.

"*Abee*, did you miss us?"

29

"What did you see?"

"May we visit the cave sometime?"

"Are you home for a few days?"

"Did you bring us something special from your mountain?"

Khadija laughed. Leaning against the doorway, she watched the happy reunion. To the children, even a few days away from their father was an eternity. Looking at him play with their daughters, she knew that his spiritual depth shaped his serene character, the reason she had been drawn to him years ago. Muhammad needed times of solitude, always returning to the cave on the Mountain of Light.

Khadija gazed down at their sleeping infant, Fatima, swaddled in the crook of her arm. She tucked in a corner of cloth that had loosened. Looking at the baby brought her tears of both thanks and sorrow. Sometimes the babe reminded her of her firstborn, Qasim. He had not lived long past infancy. Khadija rocked Fatima ever so slightly, as if filling her with a prayer for a long and healthy life.

Muhammad peeked over the girls' heads at his wife and smiled. Khadija beamed back and then turned to attend to the last details of dinner. Expecting his return today, she and the servants prepared a feast of lamb stew, bread, and a cucumber salad. She laid the baby on the sleeping mat in the care of a servant and walked back outside to the courtyard and fire pit. The barley dough still needed attention. She kneaded the dough with the heels of her hands until it softened, then formed it into small balls between her palms and rolled them out into small discs.

Khadija took a deep breath, remembering how much had changed in her life since she had heard of "the trustworthy one" and tested his trustworthiness for herself. Wiping a bead of sweat from her brow, she knew that other people considered them an unusual couple—Khadija the elder, Muhammad the younger. Perhaps, she thought, precisely because of this difference in age and experience, he consulted her before anyone else on all serious matters.

When she thought about the women she'd seen whose husbands ruled them through brute strength, she felt especially thankful. Her relationship with Muhammad overturned a number of traditions: She was not his property, and her wealth belonged only to her. Further, he did not shy away from the household work of women and servants—he liked to mend his own clothes and sandals.

She looked up and watched Muhammad dote on the children. This too set him apart. In much of Arabia, men valued sons over daughters so much that girls were sometimes killed at birth. Muhammad found the custom intolerable.

The flatbread browned and steaming, Khadija clapped her hands to signal that dinner was ready. Muhammad tickled the girls as they shrieked with joy and pulled their father along.

The Angel

On the Mountain of Light, from the mouth of his cave, Muhammad watched heat waves snake skyward from the desert floor. The rocks and desert appeared colorless, as did the sky. The wind had stilled. Birds, hiding in the few acacia trees, suspended their songs.

Muhammad sat alone in the cave's shade, his breath echoing off its rounded walls. No longer a young man, he had continued coming to this sanctuary during the fifteen years of his marriage. But this time, the solitude and prayer brought the strangest nights of his life: More and more, his dreams were filled with a mysterious light. Talking with Khadija about it had reassured him, but here, isolated in the desert, the radiance of his dreams grew.

Suddenly, an overwhelming presence, an angel, grabbed him. He heard a voice intone, "Peace be upon you, Messenger of God!"

Startled and terrified, Muhammad then heard, "Recite!

Read!"

He could neither read nor write, so Muhammad answered, "I am not of those who read!"

The angel squeezed Muhammad tighter. "Recite! Read!"

Muhammad answered again, "I am not of those who read!"

It pressed upon him so forcefully he thought he would choke. "Recite! Read!" repeated the voice a third time. "Recite: In the Name of your Lord Who created, created man from a blood-clot. Recite: and your Lord is the Most Generous, Who taught by the pen—taught man what he did not know."

Muhammad trembled with fear and recited the words the angel spoke. Then as mysteriously as the angel appeared, the angel left, but Muhammad later said, "It was as though the words were written on my heart." He would never forget them. Shaking, looking around at the now-empty desert, Muhammad wondered if jinn, the genies of the desert, had attacked him. Did something devilish possess him? What happened? He searched the distance of the empty desert. Only miles of silence responded to his pounding heart.

Muhammad decided he must return home and talk with Khadija. Perhaps she could explain what had occurred. He gathered his few belongings—a blanket, the water left in his goatskin, dates—and rushed away. Yet he hadn't gone far when he heard a voice above him boom, "Oh Muhammad, thou art the Messenger of God, and I am

Gabriel." Looking up, Muhammad saw the angel outspread from one end of the horizon to the other. When he turned in another direction, there, too, the angel filled the horizon. He hurried home, fastening his gaze on the stones and sand between the mountain and Mecca.

Arriving there a short time later, Muhammad begged Khadija, "Cover me! Cover me!" She led him to their sleeping cot and wrapped him in a cloak. She had never seen Muhammad like this—he was known for his composure.

After describing the experience in the cave, Muhammad asked, "What is happening to me? I fear for myself!"

Holding him, she whispered, "You have nothing to fear. Have a rest and calm down. God will not let you suffer any humiliation: You are kind to your kinsfolk, you speak the truth, you help those in need . . . and you support every just cause," Khadija reassured him. Muhammad acted honorably in every situation, so this remarkable experience could not be a deception.

She hung a cloak over the window to block the glaring sun so he might rest. When Muhammad's breath eased from the fitful state, she held his hand and watched.

After a time, she decided to visit her old and blind cousin Waraqah, a Christian, who lived nearby. He had knowledge of the great Prophets—Abraham, Isaiah, Jesus, and others. Was her husband also a Prophet? Waraqah would know. It was unusual to pay a visit while the sun still seared, but this couldn't be put off.

She told Zaynab to let Father rest and charged her with the care of the younger children while she hastened toward Waraqah's home.

Khadija thumped on her cousin's door. It opened a crack and then swung wide. Waraqah could sense that Khadija had come with a serious purpose. Walking into the courtyard, out of hearing from the street, they settled on cushions in the shade of a wall. Without delay, Khadija described the angel's presence and the words Muhammad heard at the cave. Waraqah leaned forward and listened closely, his eyes rounding in wonder. He had been waiting for a Prophet of God to appear for the Arab people.

Waraqah grabbed both of Khadija's hands in his own, exclaiming, "Holy, holy, holy!" He looked in her direction and said, "Indeed, Muhammad is the Prophet of this people." Tears welled in his eyes, and he bowed his head in prayer. After some time in silence, Khadija stood and let herself out, closing the door softly behind. She returned home and repeated what Waraqah said to Muhammad, assuring him that he should finish the days of Ramadan on the Mountain of Light.

Muhammad did as Waraqah suggested. Later, when he returned to Mecca, he went straight to the Kaaba. Among those sitting nearby was Waraqah, who was anxious to hear any news from Muhammad. "Tell me, what you have seen and heard?" Waraqah asked.

Muhammad told him, word for word, about the experiences on the mountain. In the same way he had reassured Khadija, Waraqah affirmed Muhammad's role as a Messenger of God. Waraqah then sat in thoughtful silence for some moments. Watching the old man's face, Muhammad waited. Suddenly, Waraqah looked up and warned Muhammad, "You will certainly be called a liar and be ill-treated. They will banish you and make war upon you!" Waraqah paused to let Muhammad think on this. "Your people will turn you away!"

Muhammad paled. Everyone knew the risk of losing clan protection. Only a network of close relations could meet the challenge of getting enough food and water in this harsh climate. It was the key to life. As if he hadn't heard his cousin-in-law correctly, Muhammad asked in disbelief, "Will they turn me away?"

"Indeed they will!" said Waraqah. "No man has ever brought what you have brought and not been treated as an enemy!" He kissed Muhammad on the forehead and said, "Would that I live to see that day, God knows I will defend you."

Companions

After Muhammad returned home, the powerful experiences recurred. Often they came to him when he prayed, but sometimes the Angel Gabriel arrived quite unexpected—startling him out of sleep with the sound of a chime or disrupting a minor chore in the day.

Muhammad, having a business to manage and a family to raise, found it impossible to live exactly as before. No longer could he be concerned with simply earning a living, or focusing solely on the welfare of his clan. He knew that the revelations were for all humankind.

He memorized and recited the earliest revelations to Khadija. She in turn memorized and recited them. The growing collection was called the Quran. Like the Jews and Christians who followed the God of Abraham instead of the tribal gods, Muhammad and Khadija were *muslim*— they submitted in whole-hearted trust to One God. Faith in God had built the Kaaba long ago, yet over time, the holy site became the place of worship for a hundred different man-made statues, gods, beliefs, and laws.

Muhammad soon told his closest friends and family but asked them to keep it a secret. The revelations proclaimed a single God; because of this, they forbade the worship of the tribal idols at the Kaaba. If the powerful clans discovered these new ideas and rules, all the converts would be in grave trouble: The Kaaba was not only the spiritual center of Arabia; it also allowed Mecca to remain a center of trade.

The number of Believers grew by a handful of converts each week. They called themselves Muhammad's Companions. Through the revelations, God was their educator, their *Rabb*. Muhammad told them, "Seeking knowledge is the duty of every Believer. It will enable you to be your own friend in the desert, it will be your mainstay in solitude, your companion in loneliness, your guide to happiness, your sustainer in misery."

Twice a day now, in the morning and in the evening, small groups met in secret for worship. Some walked in groups of two or three into the desert so they would not be seen; some met with Muhammad in the house of a Companion where a new revelation could be memorized and explained.

When Mecca slipped out of the sun's grasp and stars freckled the eastern horizon, the first soft knock on a Companion's front door opened it just enough to let in a single person at a time. "*As-salaam alaykum*, peace be upon you," said Ali, entering. He was Muhammad's first cousin and one of the first Companions.

"*Wa alaykum as-salaam*, and with you also," replied the host, smiling—this was the greeting of peace that Gabriel taught Muhammad. The last of a small group arriving for worship, Ali locked the door behind himself. In the waning light of the courtyard, unseen and unheard from the street, Muhammad's Companions formed lines and knelt on palm mats in order to pray.

Muhammad and Khadija needed to be watchful. The revelations would spin the world of the powerful in Mecca upside down. Not only had Muhammad declared a belief in One God—the statues at the Kaaba were nothing more than statues he said—but also the money from religious pilgrims for food, water, and housing while in Mecca kept the large and powerful Quraysh tribe, the guardians of the shrine, very rich.

Additionally, Muhammad taught that all people, wealthy or poor, were equal before God, "as equal as the teeth of a comb," he said, and the rich had a duty to share their wealth with the poor. A revelation that would further upset the powerful stated that the oppressed must be freed: Women were men's partners, not property; infant girls must not be killed; slaves must be able to earn their freedom.

Arabia would never be the same if these ideas took

hold.

Muhammad began to worship—reciting the words of praise soundlessly. He was pleased to see his Companions doing the same thing. One by one, they finished praying, and settled into a kneeling pose on the mat, ready to learn a new revelation.

On this night, Muhammad decided to teach some verses from the Quran that express the evidence of Allah's presence everywhere. More than anything, Muhammad felt that his mission was to help people remember their dependence on God in all things and at all times, in this life and beyond.

Muhammad began, "In the name of God, the Compassionate, the Merciful." Whenever Khadija heard those words, she felt great comfort. Every chapter of the Quran began like this. One of the names for God, Ar-Rahman, the Most Kind and Compassionate, was especially dear to her husband who had named a new Companion with it just yesterday, Abdur-Rahman, servant of the Most Kind.

Muhammad spoke:

And of His signs is that He created you of dust, then lo! you are human beings, spreading. And of His signs is that He created for you from yourselves mates that you might find peace by their side, and He ordained between you affection and mercy. Surely in that there are signs for a people who reflect . . .

And of His signs is the creation of the heavens and
the earth and the differences of your tongues and

Muhammad continued,

And of His signs is His showing you lightning to
arouse fear and hope, and He sends down water
from the heaven and with it He revives the earth
after it has died.

When finished, Muhammad gazed at the Companions
and said, "Surely in that there are signs for people who
understand." He smiled. Now the group would memorize
the revelations as Muhammad had. Like their nomadic
forefathers and mothers who carried no books, Arabs were
masters in memorizing long passages of poetry, story, and
history. They would practice these verses with Muhammad until every word was exactly right.

Muhammad began again, "In the name of God, the
Compassionate, the Merciful." The Companions followed,
chanting word by word. Their voices together surged,
dipped and pooled like water rushing down from mountains.

When finished, their hosts invited them to settle on
camel-leather cushions scattered around the courtyard or
lean against the cool walls of thick mud brick. It was time
for explanations of the latest revelations and for Muham-

mad to answer questions.

Servants soon appeared and offered the guests some water, dried dates, and raisins. Then unlike anywhere else in Mecca, and perhaps unlike anywhere else in the world, those servants who believed in the truth of Muhammad's message sat right alongside their masters to learn from their new teacher.

Not for the Sun

The Quraysh were furious. Several of the tribe's nobles stood at the edge of the small crowd that clustered around Muhammad to hear a sermon near the Kaaba. This wasn't the first time he'd gathered people around him to announce his message. A wealthy visitor strode by and entered the building, his silks catching the sun like so many jewels. In a soft voice, Muhammad said to his followers, "Wealth is not the possession of goods; wealth is the wealth of the soul." Muhammad nodded toward the crowd in front of him—some of the poorest in Mecca, hungry for food as well as Muhammad's message—and led them in a short prayer:

> He is God, One!
> God, the Self-Sufficient, Besought of all.
> He neither begot, nor was begotten.
> Nor is there anyone equal to Him.

Enraged at this impudence right in front of the Kaaba, the Quraysh nobles turned and spoke among themselves in raised voices. No longer was Muhammad's message a secret from his fellow Meccans. Only last week, he had arranged feasts of lamb and addressed the nobles directly with news of the revelations. His boldness still burned in their minds. "I know of no Arab who has come to his people with a nobler message than mine," he had said. "God has commanded me to call you to Him. Which of you will help me with this . . . ?" Except for the promise of thirteen-year-old Ali—Muhammad's beloved cousin—he had faced stony silence.

"This *has* to end!" said a noble, looking from Muhammad to the others. "Now Muhammad dares to scorn the statues and their visitors right in front of the Kaaba!" His face reddened. "If people listen to this nonsense, they will stop coming to Mecca; they will take their gods and business elsewhere." The assembled Quraysh all began speaking at once: Muhammad must be stopped.

They set out to speak with Abu Talib, young Ali's father, as well as Muhammad's uncle and protector. They hastened to his home and demanded to speak with him right away. Although startled by their force, Abu Talib invited them into his home. The men sat themselves on cushions and wasted no time getting to the point. Abu Sufyan, one of the nobles, said it plainly, "Your nephew has insulted our gods and condemned our religion. He considers our young men to be fools, and our fathers to have erred in their beliefs. You must either restrain him or allow us free action against him."

The next day, Abu Talib decided he must see for himself. After all, he was the leader of his clan. By the time he arrived at the crowd around Muhammad, a mid-day wind had kicked up small dust devils. A few people covered their mouth and nose with scarves. Others simply squinted into the stinging sand, hoping for a few more words from Muhammad.

Abu Talib quickly took stock of the situation: Muhammad preaching in front of the Kaaba, dissuading the visitors from paying tribute there, while the Quraysh tried to make those same visitors feel welcome.

Just then Muhammad's voice carried to his uncle's ears. He was leading a prayer:

Praise be to God; Lord of all Worlds.
The Compassionate, the Merciful.
Master of the Day of Judgment.
You alone we worship, and You alone we ask for help.

Muhammad spoke only about Allah, the One God. This further infuriated the Quraysh now surrounding Abu Talib. They offered money, power, and nobility for Muhammad if he would simply cease his preaching. They implored Abu Talib, "You are aged, noble, and highly respected among us, and we have already asked you to prohibit your nephew from offending us. But you have not prohibited him, and by God, we shall not overlook his insults unless you guarantee his future good behavior. Otherwise, we shall fight both him and you."

Deeply pained, Abu Talib was left speechless. The Quraysh threatened nothing less than bloodshed.

When the crowd dispersed, the uncle led Muhammad homeward. Arriving at Abu Talib's house, the house of Muhammad's youth, they secluded themselves in the courtyard where outsiders could not hear them speak.

Abu Talib was deeply grieved, but he would not surrender or desert Muhammad. He had raised Muhammad since his grandfather had died. Weary and sad, Abu Talib told Muhammad all that the Quraysh had said. Then he implored his nephew, "Consider my life and yours, Muhammad, and do not burden me with what I cannot bear."

Muhammad feared that his uncle, being old and weak, had decided to abandon him and side with the Quraysh. Hugging Abu Talib, he then sat back and looked him in the eye. "Oh my uncle," said Muhammad. "I swear to God that, should they place the sun in my right hand and the moon in my left hand, I would not abandon my mission." Tears flooded Muhammad's eyes. He did not wish to see his uncle suffer for him.

When at last Muhammad stood to depart, Abu Talib said, "Son of my brother! Go, and speak what you wish. By Allah! I shall never fail you."

Raise the Dead!

They were ridiculing him; he could hear them just outside the Kaaba's entrance. Ignoring the Quraysh who followed him here, Muhammad continued to pray. They had stepped up their harassment: Someone threw sheep intestines on him while he prayed in public; another had tied a cloak around his neck while he was bowed in prayer, hoping to suffocate him.

Muhammad would heed his own advice that he had given to the Believers: "Bear with patience what they say, and part from them with a courteous farewell." Inside the Kaaba, the soft light lingered through the day, and the walls muffled the sounds from the street. Muhammad found the sanctuary soothing. He stood in place, then bent at the waist, kneeled and bowed until the woven leaves of palm on the floor touched his brow.

He sat back up and took a deep breath. *Insha'Allah*—God willing—he could face the day's challenges from the

Quraysh. But what about the Companions, and especially those others without the protection of a powerful uncle or clan? The Quraysh harassed and abused Muhammad, but they tormented the powerless. Abu Bakr, Muhammad's closest friend, had already bought the freedom of six slaves—Companions—suffering for their beliefs.

Muhammad couldn't shake the latest news, however: Bilal, another slave, was being tortured for converting. Last night, a Companion burst into the evening prayer group and recounted the story: "I saw Bilal's master beating and prodding him through the streets of Mecca, so I stayed out of sight and followed," he said. "When the master reached the desert hills, he staked Bilal out in the sun, placed a large boulder on his stomach, and promised it would stay until he renounced the One God!" The Companions gasped. "As I snuck away, all I heard Bilal say to his master was, 'God is One. God is One. God is One.'"

Muhammad's eyes welled thinking about it, yet he also realized that from these torments, the Believers were uniting, looking out for one another. Later he would offer these words of comfort to the Companions: "You see the Believers being merciful among themselves, showing love and being kind, resembling one body, so that if any part of the body is not well, then the whole body shares the pain."

Muhammad rose and made his way through a maze of visitors inside the Kaaba. Many prayed while kneeling on the floor; others worshipped their gods while standing. Muhammad watched a strikingly tall man—probably a tribal chief—make an offering of dates and honey to a statue. Another pilgrim, old and stooped, fanned a wisp of smoke rising from a bowl full of spice incense. The Kaaba smelled fragrant.

Muhammad noted more than the usual number of visitors. It was nearing the time of year when all tribes of Arabia sent pilgrims to the Kaaba. The Quraysh had already received a large caravan of fruits and vegetables from Yemen in order to prepare vast amounts of food for the pilgrims.

No wonder the Quraysh followed him here today, Muhammad thought. They anticipated that he would preach to the pilgrims. In fact, unbeknownst to Muhammad, the Quraysh had posted guards on all the roads entering Mecca. They were to warn people that Muhammad was a powerful sorcerer and could split families apart. They ordered all visitors to refrain from listening to, or speaking with, Muhammad Ibn Abdullah.

When Muhammad stepped outside, the Quraysh men encircled him. Muhammad took little notice. The group followed him, jeering. They wanted solid proof that he was God's messenger. Could his Lord do something to make their lives easier? One shouted, "Ask your Lord to remove these mountains which hem us in, or ask him to flatten our land and to make rivers flow through it like the rivers of Syria and Iraq!" The men laughed, slapping each other on the back.

Another shouted, "Raise from the dead some of our forefathers . . . that we may ask them if what you say is true or false!"

A heckler said, "Or if you will not do these things for us, then ask favors for yourself! Ask God . . . to give you gardens and palaces and treasures of gold and silver! Then we'll know how well you stand with your Lord!"

A young man stepped on the back of Muhammad's robe to stop him. Muhammad turned to face the group. Calmly, he replied, "I am not one to ask of my Lord the like of such things, nor was I sent for that, but God has sent me to warn and give good tidings." He tugged his robe from under the young man's foot and walked away.

The men scrambled to keep up with him. "We swear by God," said one, "that we will not leave you in peace nor desist from our present treatment of you until we destroy you, or until you destroy us!" Muhammad did not respond; he put one foot in front of the other and continued home.

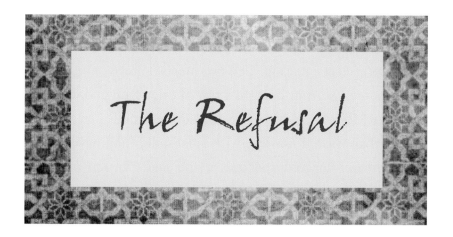

The Refusal

Even as the head of the Banu Hashim clan, Abu Talib found it harder and harder to safeguard Muhammad. Not only did the poor listen to Muhammad's new religion, but also the young of some of the wealthiest families declared themselves Believers. Fathers discovered their sons and daughters reciting verses in secret. Women and the powerless learned to read the Quran, and Muhammad encouraged them to teach others. The Believers were living by new laws. If people continued to join Muhammad's followers, tribal laws would no longer dictate society.

Before Muhammad and the Quraysh came to blows, Utbah, a Quraysh leader, was asked to try one last time to dissuade Muhammad from spreading his new religion.

The day the two men decided to meet was overcast, large clouds rolling by like threatening armies. Arriving at Utbah's home, Muhammad followed the servants into a room off the courtyard, shaded and cool. He addressed

Utbah in the manner the Angel Gabriel had taught: "*As-salam alaykum*, peace be upon you." Utbah stood but did not return the greeting. The two men sat down on leather cushions. A servant brought a tray of dried fruit and water, placed it between them, and then disappeared.

Utbah wasted no time with small talk. "You have disturbed our concord and peace," he said. "Listen to my proposal and consider it." Just then, the first raindrops in months began to fall. The men paused to watch them land in the courtyard like small explosions in the dust. Utbah turned back to Muhammad and continued, "If property be your desire, we Quraysh shall make you the richest of us; if dignity be your goal, we shall make you our prince so that nothing will be decided without you." His voice rising, Utbah finally offered all he could: "If you want to be a king, we shall make you our king!"

The rain began a steady patter. Utbah leaned in, speaking more softly: "If this be a spirit who visits you and you are unable to repel it, we shall find a physician and give him money till he cures you of it!"

Muhammad listened. After a time, he answered Utbah by reciting several long verses from the Quran. Despite the deplorable things Utbah had heard about Muhammad's religion, he found the chanted words astonishing and wonderful. Muhammad completed a final verse:

And among His signs are the night and the day, and

the sun and the moon. Do not prostrate to the sun and moon, but prostrate to God Who created them, if it is Him Whom you worship.

Finishing, Muhammad bowed, resting his forehead on the ground. Utbah, speechless, blanched. Deeply shaken, he felt drained of any resolve to persuade Muhammad to abandon the new religion. Muhammad stood, leaving Utbah without an answer to the offers made by the Quraysh.

When Utbah reported back to the other nobles, they were struck by his change in expression and shocked with his conclusion. "What has happened to you?" they asked.

"I have heard an utterance the likes of which I have never yet heard. It is not poetry, by God, neither is it sorcery or soothsaying. Men of Quraysh, listen to me, and do as I say. Come not between this man and what he is about, for by God, the words that I have heard from him will be received as great tidings."

"Ha!" they laughed. "He has bewitched you!"

"No," said Utbah, gesturing dismissively. "I have given you my opinion, so do what you think is best."

As Utbah brought no answer from Muhammad, the Quraysh decided to make the offers again, this time as a group. "Let us send for Muhammad and talk and argue with him, so that we cannot be blamed for having left any way to avoid bloodshed untried."

Muhammad, receiving word that the nobles wanted to speak with him, hoped that the Quraysh had changed their minds and were now receptive to his message. He hurried to them, but they only repeated the offers made by Utbah hours ago. Muhammad, deep in thought, listened without responding.

After a time, Muhammad said to the Quraysh, "I am not possessed, nor do I seek among you honors or power." He surveyed the group of men. "God has sent me to you as a messenger; He has revealed to me a Book and has ordered me to bring you good news and warn you." He paused, letting the words take effect. "If you accept from me what I have brought you, that is your good fortune in this world and the next; but if you reject what I have brought, then will I patiently await God's judgment between us."

Stunned, the men dissolved into shouted taunts aimed at Muhammad. Among the most respected and wealthy tribes of all Arabia, they had offered Muhammad the lion's share of their worldly goods and power. His refusal was an outrageous humiliation. It was also an invitation to war.

The First to Flight

They took off in small groups in the dark over several weeks' time, traveling at night, crossing the Red Sea, and hoping that the absence of eighty kinsmen would not be discovered until their safe arrival in Abyssinia.

The Quraysh refused to let up on the most vulnerable Companions—the poorest—so Muhammad had suggested that some young men and women migrate south. The Christian king there, the Negus, might allow them to worship freely. It was a gamble, but after all, the Believers and the Christians worshipped the same God, the God of Abraham. Surely the Negus would protect them.

Muhammad chose his own daughter, Ruqayyah and her husband, Uthman, as part of the leadership. Their presence would demonstrate his depth of commitment. Some refugees left Mecca because they suffered too much; some who were learned in the verses of the Quran chose to join them; some whose eloquence could explain their religion to others added to their numbers. For one and all, the decision to leave all they knew in life—their families, their clans and their city—was a great sacrifice.

When the Quraysh finally realized their kinsmen had disappeared for the freedom of the Abyssinian Empire, they panicked. What if the group attracted more and more converts? What if they rallied the Abyssinians against the tribal gods? What if Muhammad and his followers became so powerful that they threatened Mecca's role as the religious and trading center of Arabia? The Quraysh could not take this chance.

Quickly, they hatched a plan. It was known that the Abyssinian nobles revered fine leather—the specialty of Mecca—so they gathered the finest skins in the city for gifts. They chose Amr from the clan of Sahm and another envoy to carry it out. The two men planned to meet first with the Abyssinian generals, lavish them with presents, and then persuade them of the Muslims' mistaken ways. By the time Amr met with the king, the generals would surely help him argue his cause. The two Qurayshi hurried south by camel, west by boat, then climbed into the high country of the capital, Axum.

Cool, crisp, mountain air met them on their first morning in the city of Axum. Amr stared out his window, transfixed by hillsides covered with the emerald patchwork of lush meadows and dense forests. He walked through the door of his room onto grass glinting with dew from the night. To desert eyes, this land was stunning. Eventually, he broke his gaze and woke his companion. They would need to dress in their best for an audience with the first of the Abyssinian generals.

When the general's servant arrived, the envoys followed him through winding city streets. A bazaar full of unfamiliar fruits and vegetables caught Amr's eye, as did the stalls of elephant ivory and Indian silks. They passed a church carved of white pumice and finally arrived at an imposing mansion of both rough and cut stone.

After Amr completed the formal greetings, he presented the general with ten fine camel skins and then spoke his case: "Some foolish young men and women of our people have taken refuge in your kingdom," he said. "They have left their own religion, not for yours but for one they have invented, one that is unknown to us or to you. The nobles of their people have sent us to your king on their account, that he may send them home." The general, fingering the stack of gifts, continued to listen. "So when we speak to your king," said Amr, "please counsel him to deliver our people into our hands and have no words with them. Their own people know what is best for them."

One after the other, after receiving a pile of fine leather from the Quraysh, each general agreed with the envoys— what Amr said made perfect sense. Soon enough, the Quraysh requested an audience with the Negus, the king.

A few days later, the two envoys arrived at the royal palace. Flanked by several guards, they were led through the palace gates, through another fortified wall, and into the castle keep. At the far end of a large carpeted hall, the Negus sat on a sturdy throne atop a dais, dressed in white linen robes, wearing a gold crown and a dozen gold bracelets.

The Quraysh, whose forefathers were desert nomads, surveyed the great hall, astounded by the wealth and power the Negus had amassed. Amr, remembering his promise to the tribal council, took a deep breath. He then approached the king with a formal greeting and spoke, explaining the situation of the young refugees. He ended his speech with a request: "The nobles of their people, who are their fathers, their uncles, and their kinsmen, beg you to return their children and kin to them."

Amr eyed the line of seated generals. Before the king could speak, they joined in, trying to convince the Negus to return the Believers, arguing that their families knew them best and were the best judges of their own affairs.

After a short time, the king would hear no more. He raised his palm to quiet them and said, "Nay, by God, they shall not be betrayed!" His face froze into a stern mask. "A people who have sought my protection and made my country their home and chosen me above all others! I will not give them up until I have questioned them myself."

He looked at his generals with scorn. "If it is as the Quraysh say, then I will return them to their own people. But if not, then I will be their good protector so long as they want it."

The envoys had dearly hoped that the refugees would not be allowed an audience with the king. Amr clasped his hands behind his back and cast his eyes downward, hiding his disappointment. While the men and women from Mecca were summoned, the king's bishops entered the hall carrying their holy Bibles, and laid them out on a table in front of the Negus. They, too, would judge this new religion of the refugees.

When the refugees filed in, several of the nobles and bishops began to whisper among themselves, struck that the young men and women dressed modestly and their manners were pious and humble. When the group at last stood before the Negus, he asked, "What is this religion that has separated you from your people, though you have not entered my religion nor that of any of the surrounding folk?"

Ja'far, the most eloquent among them said, "O King, we were a people steeped in ignorance and worshipping idols. The strong would devour the weak." He glanced briefly in the direction of Amr. "Then God sent us a Messenger from out of our midst, one whose ancestors we knew, as well as his truthfulness, worthiness, and integrity." Ja'far paused and then continued, "He called us unto God, that we should testify to his Oneness and worship Him and renounce what we and our fathers had worshipped in the way of stones and idols."

His words rang uninterrupted in the great hall's silence. Ja'far pressed on: "He commanded us to speak truly, to fulfill our promises, to respect the ties of kinship and the rights of our neighbors, and to refrain from crimes and from bloodshed." Ja'far looked at the bishops. "So we worship God alone, setting nothing above Him, forbidding what He has forbidden, and following His laws. For these reasons have our people turned against us, and have persecuted us to make us forsake our religion and revert from the worship of God to the worship of idols."

Ja'far turned back to face the king. "That is why we have come to your country and chosen you above all others. We have been happy in your protection, and it is our hope, O King, that here, with you, we shall not suffer anymore."

The king's interpreters translated what had been said, and the king then asked if they could recite any of the revelations of their Prophet Muhammad for him. Since the king was a Christian, Ja'far recited a teaching in the Quran about Mary, the mother of Jesus. An angel had appeared to Mary and told her she would give birth to a holy son. She asked,

How shall I have a boy when no human being has ever touched me, neither have I been unchaste?

The angel said,

It shall be so! Your Lord has said: "It is easy for Me, and so that We may make him a sign for mankind, and a mercy from Us. And it is a thing already decreed." *

As Ja'far chanted these words in Arabic, the bishops and the Negus wept, and they wept again when it was translated for them. At last, Ja'far finished reciting. He bowed his head, and waited for the king's reaction. In the background, uncertain of their fate, the small group of refugees spoke their prayers for the king's protection noiselessly.

The silence seemed to stretch the full length of the hall and expand upward to the highest corners. At last, the Negus looked ready to address all those assembled in the great hall. Radiant and without a flicker of doubt, the king pronounced, "These words have truly come from the same source as Jesus."

Turning to the envoys of the Quraysh, he sternly spoke, "You may leave, for by God, I will not give them to you and they shall not be betrayed."

Before the Negus could see his face redden with rage, Amr dropped his head in a bow. He stood still until his breath slowed, then gave a sidelong glance to the other envoy. Without a word, both men hastened out of the great hall.

* *The belief in the One God is central to Islam, yet the Quran often uses various pronouns including "We" and "Our." They are simply a style of speech—the exact words spoken by the Angel Gabriel to convey Allah's power, majesty, and glory.*

The Boycott

People parted as the men made their way toward the Kaaba: Never before had so many Quraysh nobles—over forty of them—gathered together to walk in a show of strength through the streets. In control of Mecca for many generations, the Quraysh—their gods and their rules—commanded the city. They refused to see it torn in two by the man Muhammad, who called himself Messenger of God.

Starting today, they would enact a new strategy to quash him. Because Muhammad's Companions came from every clan in Mecca, the Quraysh decided to fall back on a basic tribal creed: If Muhammad were the source of trouble, his clan needed punishing. All of the Hashimites would suffer equally with Muhammad whether they had converted or not. Kinsmen are responsible for their own.

By the time the solemn line of nobles reached the Kaaba, many curious onlookers trailed behind. When the

Quraysh leaders went inside, a large group pressed from the outside. "What is the occasion?" some asked.

"What has happened to bring them all together today?" others wondered. No one seemed to know the answer. But as the sun beat down, their interest began to change to impatience.

Barely in time to quell the throng, a speaker stepped from the entrance of the Kaaba and unrolled a parchment. He read the proclamation loudly and slowly, so that every word rang out: "No buying from, or selling to a Hashimite; no marrying a Hashimite woman, or giving one's daughter in marriage to a Hashimite; no social or economic interaction with Muhammad's clan in any way."

When he finished, the Quraysh nobles took the new laws—penned on smooth goatskin—from the speaker. They posted them inside the Kaaba where no one—local or visiting pilgrim—could escape their words or their seriousness.

On the outskirts of the crowd, Abu Talib, Muhammad's uncle and vowed protector, heard the proclamation clearly. He shook his head in despair. Because he chose to be loyal to his nephew, others would endure the same hardship as Muhammad. Abu Talib realized that his family's fortunes would soon change drastically. He turned toward home, heavy with thought. Nothing good could come of these new laws—only great suffering for many.

The Prophet of Arabia

By and by, the Banu Hashim clan found themselves living in a small enclave on the outskirts of Mecca. Abu Talib had ordered everyone onto his land so they could protect themselves and share food more efficiently. The Quraysh posted guards to enforce the boycott. No one could enter the enclave to bring in supplies, nor leave in order to fetch goods.

All too soon, men, women, and children found themselves eating shreds of animal fodder, leather, and thorny desert plants. Daily, only a few camel skins of water snuck past the Quraysh. Abu Bakr, who was from a different clan and Muhammad's dearest friend, spent most of his wealth smuggling in items to keep the community alive.

Over time, unable to purchase food or buy water in the open bazaar, the clan suffered and sickened. Often, when a child wailed with hunger, her family possessed nothing to help. Some found that sucking on small stones kept the mouth wet and distracted from thirst. Elders, already weak with age, found that they could no longer rise from their pallets on the floor. Yet through all this, steeped in his faith in Allah, Muhammad encouraged the community of Believers, the *ummah*, saying,

Truly with hardship comes ease.

The Companions continued to gather twice a day to pray. Without water, they performed *wudu*, the purification before worship, with sand. They persevered, writing and memorizing the revelations. Looking at their suffering, Muhammad reminded them again and again that God's peace lights the way forward through every challenge.

God is the Protector of the believers; He brings them forth from the shadows into the light.

Although the ban took a terrible toll on the two clans and many perished, neither Muhammad nor his Companions had given up their religion as the Quraysh had hoped. The boycott failed completely. Perhaps even worse for the Quraysh, the ban brought more and more attention across Arabia to the man who many now called the Prophet of the Arabs—the Prophet Muhammad ﷺ.

ﷺ *denotes the phrase "peace be upon him," which Muslims say when they refer to the Prophet Muhammad* ﷺ *.*

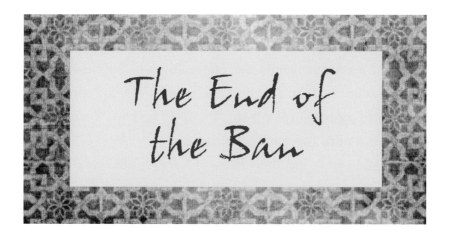

The End of the Ban

After two years or so, many Meccans longed for an end to the cruel boycott. Tribal members divided from their extended kin by the ban could not bear to see them suffer further. The situation had to change. Three leading clansmen called for a tribal council at the Kaaba. Zuhayr, one of Muhammad's cousins who was firmly against continuing the ban, was their spokesman.

For such an important meeting, Zuhayr sanctified himself in the traditional way—donning a long white robe and then circling the Kaaba seven times. He stood outside the Kaaba door, watching the men as they began to assemble. Although it was mid-morning and not yet hot, he helped the eldest among them find places to sit in the shade. The meeting might last a long time. His group would not leave until all the clans agreed to end the boycott.

Zuhayr stood, faced the assembled, and waited for them to quiet. "O people of Mecca," he began. "Are we to eat food and wear clothes, while the sons of Hashim perish, unable to buy and unable to sell?" He looked over the crowd, letting his words take effect. Almost all of them had at least one relative caught in the boycott's web. Pounding fist into palm, his voice rose: "By God," he said, "I will not sit down until this evil ban is torn up!"

Right away, the men began to argue, elbowing each other and shouting to be heard. Finally Abu Jahl, an uncle of Muhammad who was in favor of the ban, pointed at Zuhayr, shouting, "You lie! It shall not be torn up!"

The argument quickly fractured the Quraysh—some insisted that an end to the ban would doom Mecca's future. Other Qurayshis were ready to risk their livelihoods to end the boycott. Lost in the skirmish, Zuhayr's voice dissolved into the crowd. At last, fed up with the clamor, one of the men ran inside the Kaaba to get the proclamation. He discovered only a shred of it remained. He paused—surely this was a sign from God. He rushed outside and waved it at the assembled, beaming. One by one, the men hushed. They could see for themselves: Worms had eaten the vellum banner. All that remained were the opening words, "In Thy Name, O God." The assembled agreed to abandon the boycott and the Quraysh and the Believers crafted a fragile truce between them.

Year of Sorrow

It would be known as the Year of Sorrow. Although the ban had ended and a shaky truce held between the Believers and the Quraysh, many of those who suffered needed time to recover. Some would never recover.

A moth dove into the candle flame in Muhammad and Khadija's room, its burning wings flicking spectral shapes against the mud walls. On the bed, weak from the years of hunger, Khadija lay dying. Muhammad sat beside her, propping her head into the curve of his arm. She was too frail to hold it aloft herself. Their youngest, Fatima, kneeled beside her mother on the other side, tears falling steadily. Two other daughters, Zaynab and Umm Kulthum, stood at the foot of the bed quietly weeping. Ruqayyah, still in Abyssinia, would miss her mother's passing.

Gazing down at Khadija, Muhammad traced the strands of hair, now gilded silver, and knew that she was yet another sign of Allah's goodness, perhaps the most important in his life. Khadija had been the first to recognize Muhammad as a Messenger of God. There was no question that her willingness to share his persecution and to spend her fortune taking care of the *ummah*, the community, allowed Muhammad's message to flourish. Gently, he hugged her. So many times he had said, "Women are the twin halves of men." He looked at Zaynab's husband in the corner of the room and said, "They are your garments as you are their garments."

Muhammad could barely imagine life without Khadija. Yet both had found ultimate solace in their faith: They both knew that the gift of her life, as well as his, had always depended on Allah.

After Khadija's death, the Year of Sorrow continued—both for the Companions and for Muhammad. The beleaguered community needed to mend. Restoring flocks of sheep, goats, and camels to their previous numbers would take years. Trade relationships with partners across the Arabian Peninsula needed rebuilding.

Sadly for Muhammad, not long after his wife's death he found himself holding the fragile hand of his treasured uncle, Abu Talib, as he took his final breaths. In the adjoining room, Muhammad's aunt and cousins spoke softly. Muhammad wiped Abu Talib's wrinkled forehead with a cool cloth and marveled at the remarkable generosity of this man. Abu Talib had fed and clothed Muhammad as one of his own children; he had secured Muhammad's future by hiring him as a shepherd and then later, training him in trade. Perhaps most astonishing of all, when the Quraysh tormented the Companions through hunger, Abu Talib, although not a convert to Muhammad's beliefs, continued to protect Muhammad and his kin.

Abu Talib exhaled one last time. Muhammad squeezed the cool, frail hand, feeling the child-thin bones. He remembered that his uncle loved a particular saying spoken by Muhammad not long ago: "Love for humanity what you love for yourself." Abu Talib's life showed he had lived Muhammad's words to the fullest.

The Vision

With the death of Abu Talib, Muhammad lost his only clan protection in Mecca. No longer would his preaching at the Kaaba be tolerated; no longer would the Quraysh beg Muhammad's Companions to stop worshipping in the open—they would make them stop.

The new truce between the Quraysh and the Believers quickly unraveled. Muhammad was abused worse than before—rotten meat was tossed into his family's cook pot and filth-covered sheep organs flew over his head while he prayed in his own courtyard. When he came out of the Kaaba, Muhammad was showered with dirt. When one of his daughters washed his face of it later, he quelled her tears saying, "Weep not, little daughter. God will protect your father."

Looking to safeguard the most vulnerable of his Companions, Muhammad ventured to the nearby town of Ta'if to invite the clan chiefs join the community of Believers and thus gain the chiefs' protection. However, they considered their religion and their shrine to the Goddess al-Lat every bit as important as the One God Muhammad spoke of and so they mocked him, laughing and saying, "Could God send no one better than you for a messenger?"

Another taunted, "Let me never speak to you again! For if you are a Messenger from God as you say, then you are too great a person for me to speak with!" and he bowed as if in front of a king. "And if you are a liar, it is not fitting to talk to you at all!" He turned his back to Muhammad, and the men guffawed. To make their point, the chiefs gathered a crowd to throw rocks and pebbles at Muhammad until he left.

Muhammad had no choice but to return to Mecca. However, he now knew his community of vulnerable Companions needed to move elsewhere—life had become intolerable for them.

Some time later, he had a dream. He saw a clear vision of a new homeland. He shared it with the Companions the following day to give them hope: "I have been shown the place of your emigration: I saw a well-watered land, rich in date palms, between two tracts of black stones."

Insha'Allah

Not long after his rejection by the chiefs of Ta'if, during the month of reflection, Muhammad met a group from the city of Yathrib, which was eleven camel days to the north. Camped in the hills around Mecca during the holy time, the six men watched Muhammad as he visited the tents of religious pilgrims from across Arabia, reciting the Quran to anyone willing to listen. But the group from Yathrib looked at Muhammad with special interest. The Jewish people of their city foretold of a coming Prophet. Was Muhammad that man?

One night, as the sun striped the western horizon with pinks and purples, the group invited Muhammad into their camp to break the day-long fast together. They wanted to know what this man calling himself a Prophet had to say.

Around a small campfire, the men sat on their heels or on flat rocks. Thirsty and hungry from a day without water or food, they passed several camel skins from one person to the next until each drank his fill. The fire's embers warmed a stew of barley and meat. When the scent wafted through the circle of men, their stomachs churned in hunger: At last it was time to eat.

Later, as the stars brightened in the darkening sky, Muhammad spoke about the peace found in recognizing our dependence on God, Allah. Reciting the words of the Quran exactly as Gabriel had spoken them to him, he said,

> The One Who made for you the earth a cradle, and threaded for you therein ways, and sent down from the heaven water. And therewith We brought forth various kinds of plants . . . . From it We created you, and into it We shall restore you, and from it We shall bring you forth a second time.

Every desert dweller relied on God's blessings of earth and water to survive. As Muhammad studied the men's faces, he saw the feeling of *islam*—surrender to dependence on God—shine in their eyes. Raising his palms toward the sky, he proclaimed,

Truly, God is unfathomable in his wisdom and All-Aware. *Allahu Akbar,* God is great!"

Muhammad recited from the Quran until one by one, each man took the *Shahada,* the statement of belief: "*la ilaha illa Allahu, Muhammadun rasulu Allahi:* I believe there is no God but God, and Muhammad is the Messenger of God."

Afterward, they stared at the fire's last coals, quiet, lost in contemplation. In time, the men explained their situation in Yathrib to Muhammad. An endless blood feud between their tribe, the Khazraj, and their rivals, the Aws, had caused them to flee. No leader seemed capable of ending their civil war, and so the group intended to stay in Mecca.

"We have left our people and our city," they said to Muhammad. "For there are no people so torn in two by hatred as they." The firelight played upon the circle of faces, wearied and despondent from years of battle.

Their spokesman paused for a time, and then looked up at Muhammad. "Perhaps," he said, looking at the Prophet with a steady gaze, "God can unite them through you."

The six men looked at one another, a spark of hope in their eyes, their heads beginning to nod in agreement with this idea. When the Khazraj leader saw his men's enthusiasm, he made a pledge: "We will go to our people and ask them to accept your religion as we have accepted it; and if God gathers them together around you, then no man will be mightier than you." A silence enveloped Muhammad while he thought over this remarkable offer. Their pledge could change all of their lives forever—the Believers, as well as the various tribes of Yathrib.

At last Muhammad spoke, "*Insha'Allah*, if God wills it, *Insha'Allah*."

The Helpers

The plan would take time. Muhammad must ensure the Believers' safety in Yathrib; they needed more than a single tribe's protection. Before they could leave Mecca, the warring tribes must unite under Allah's laws and stop their bloody civil war.

The six Khazraji men returned to Yathrib and preached the message of the One God to anyone willing to listen. Person by person, the number of converts grew. A year later, the next summer, five of the Khazraji leaders returned with five more. Surprisingly, they also returned with two leaders from the Aws tribe, their life-long enemies.

The twelve made a new oath to Muhammad: "We pledge our loyalty to the Messenger of God and promise we will not worship idols, we will not steal . . . we will not kill our infant daughters, we will not lie or gossip. We will not disobey Muhammad in all that is right." This pledge to new laws over ancient customs would radically remake their tribal society. Many, they knew, would resist.

The leaders were sent back to Yathrib for yet another year, this time with one of Muhammad's Companions who would teach the Quran and explain its meanings. By the third year and third pilgrimage to Mecca, the chiefs of both tribes were Believers. Seventy-three men and two women, Aws and Khazraj both, made the pilgrimage and promised to protect with their lives any Believer who entered Yathrib.

Without that offer of refuge, the Believers in Mecca would continue to endure a life of persecution. In gratitude, Muhammad said that the early Believers from Yathrib would forever be known as "*Ansar*, the Helpers."

Flight

To avoid suspicion that every last Believer was abandoning Mecca, the Companions fled north in small groups. Many concealed their preparations from their families, who would certainly forbid their leaving. Daughters disguised themselves and stole away from their parents in the middle of the night; sons packed only what they could conceal and carry. Faith in God more than clan now guided their lives.

In time, a number of homes were left with only a few elders remaining to take care of them. Mecca, a bustling, prosperous city only ten years earlier, found itself struggling to remain the center of Arabia. Almost every Believer but Muhammad and his closest circle had escaped. Abu Bakr, his dear friend, asked to leave, but Muhammad said, "Do not hurry away, for it may be that God will give you a companion." Abu Bakr knew then that the two of them, somehow, would slip away from Mecca together. He began to fatten two camels for the trip ahead.

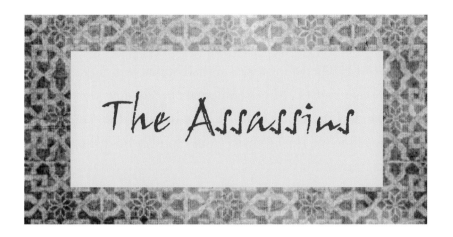

The Assassins

The Quraysh now watched Muhammad's every move: If he fled to Yathrib, it would solidify and empower enemies there. What if more and more people believed in Muhammad's religion? What if the Believers decided to prevent pilgrims from worshipping tribal gods in the Kaaba? The Quraysh would not chance it.

A tribal council decided that the clearest way to end this threat was to kill Muhammad. If each clan volunteered a young man capable of inflicting a deathblow by sword, then no single clan could be blamed. All would share the responsibility for his murder equally. But the Angel Gabriel visited Muhammad and told him of the council's decision to kill him. He advised Muhammad what to do when the day arrived.

On the night of the planned attack, as soon as darkness fell, the chosen young men gathered outside Muhammad's house as agreed. Immediately, however, they heard the voices of women inside the home—among them Fatima, Muhammad's youngest daughter, and Aisha, Muhammad's wife-to-be. The young assassins had hoped to simply enter the house and kill the troublemaker. But now they had to abandon their first plan. If they invaded the women's privacy indoors, the Quraysh would forever be dishonored across Arabia.

They came up with a new plan: Muhammad left for prayers early in the morning, so why not kill him then? When he stepped outside the house just as the sky lightened, they would set upon him.

Meanwhile, Muhammad followed the Angel Gabriel's instructions. First, he gave his cousin and son-in-law, Ali, his sleeping cloak, saying, "Sleep on my bed and wrap yourself in this green robe. Sleep in it, and no harm will come to you from the assassins." When they extinguished the lanterns and candles, Ali climbed into the bed and covered himself. Muhammad then recited a particular verse from the Quran, and when he came to the words,

And We have set before them a barrier and behind them a barrier; so We have covered them, so they do not see,

he left the house, unseen by any of the young men.

Hastening away, Muhammad passed a man farther down the street who recognized him. When the man then walked by the group of assassins waiting outside Muhammad's house with their swords at the ready, he informed them that Muhammad had escaped.

Confused and disbelieving, the young men helped to perch a spy on a neighboring roof so he could peek in Muhammad's window. A sleeping figure lay on Muhammad's sleeping mat. He climbed down quietly and whispered to the others that the man was mistaken: Muhammad lay fast asleep on his bed. They continued their vigil until dawn.

When Ali arose at dawn for prayers, he opened the front door and stepped outside. Swords raised, the group of assassins believed they'd have Muhammad alone and defenseless. Vexed by Ali's presence, the men quickly suspected a trick. Where was their enemy, Muhammad? They barged past Ali to Muhammad's sleeping mat. Empty! They looked behind every cushion and corner. Gone! After a brief and angry discussion, the young men dispersed. Each would have to face his clan chief and admit that Muhammad had vanished.

Word of Muhammad's escape spread quickly. Men all over the city grabbed swords and saddled camels. The women quickly packed food for their saddlebags and filled camel skins with water. The whole of Mecca was on alert: A fortune would be given to anyone who could find Muhammad.

The Cave

Behind Abu Bakr's house, two camels saddled with pro-
visions pulled at their tethers. They knew a journey lay
ahead. After making his way through the empty streets
of Mecca on this moonless night, Muhammad knocked
softly at the front door. Within minutes, the two men plus
Abdullah, Abu Bakr's son, slipped out a back window and
mounted the camels. They fled, trusting that Allah hid
their escape from their enemies.

Because the Quraysh knew that all the Companions had
headed north to Yathrib, Muhammad and Abu Bakr hurried
in the opposite direction—south. As they passed by the
outskirts of Mecca under the starry desert sky, Muhammad reined in his camel, Qaswa, and paused to look back
a final time, saying, "Of all God's earth, you are the dearest place to me and the dearest to God, and had not my
people driven me out from you, I would never have left."
For Muhammad, as well as the whole *ummah* of Mecca,

89

this break with homeland for the sake of faith would be declared as the Hijrah. Solemn, Muhammad faced south again and spurred Qaswa on.

Hours later as the sky lightened, the two men hid in a cave on the Mountain of Thawr. They sent Abdullah back with the camels. To confuse anyone tracking them, a shepherd—a slave that Abu Bakr freed long ago—followed them with his flock of goats, covering the camels' tracks with dozens of small hoof prints. Abdullah would return to the cave each night, bringing the latest news from Mecca.

The reports were not good: the Quraysh had offered the huge sum of a hundred camels for Muhammad's capture. Horsemen from Mecca galloped to the north, intending to overtake the slower camels used for Muhammad's escape. Searching all the roads, mountain trails, and caves on the way to Yathrib, they found no sign of Muhammad and Abu Bakr. Just to be thorough, however, one group headed south—it was well worth the effort for such a fortune in camels.

On the third day of hiding, Muhammad and Abu Bakr began to feel confident: Only the brief winging of doves outside their cave broke the mornings' long spells of silence. They deemed it now safe from the Quraysh and planned to start their journey north the next day. But at midday, well before Abdullah returned with the latest account from Mecca, the windless desert carried the voices of a search party to their ears. The voices of five or six men grew closer, and closer still. Abu Bakr began to tremble, certain that the men were headed straight toward the hiding spot. He was not wrong: The six Qurayshis stopped directly outside the cave entrance. Abu Bakr mouthed to Muhammad, "If any one of them looks at his feet, he will surely find us!"

Muhammad looked at his friend. "No," he whispered. "We are not two, but three, for do you not know God is with us?" Gazing outside, Muhammad's face was lit for a moment by the circle of light flooding the opening. He turned back to his friend and continued, "God will surely protect us."

Just then, one of the Qurayshis said, "They could not be in this cave. Look, a dove has nested here and a spider has woven a web over the entrance." Abu Bakr held his breath while the men considered the evidence. After a short discussion, they agreed to continue their search elsewhere. Listening to the men's footsteps grow distant, Muhammad looked at Abu Bakr and smiled. "God is Merciful!"

Abu Bakr's son and daughter arrived at the cave that third night with food and water for the trip to Yathrib. Coming out to greet them, Muhammad gingerly brushed the spider's web aside, and stepped over the dove in her nest, careful not to disturb either creature that, through Allah, saved their lives.

The four picked their way down the rough slope in the dark. The rocks still held the heat from a fiery summer day, but a cooling night breeze followed the men. At the bottom of the mountain, a Bedouin guide waited with the loaded camels for Muhammad and Abu Bakr. He would lead them, as only a son of the desert could, on the least-used paths to their destination.

Qaswa grumbled in recognition when she saw Muhammad. Patting her flanks and neck, he inspected the saddlebags stuffed with dates and dried goat meat. They needed enough for a journey of at least twelve camel days. Each of the travelers took a long drink from a water skin—they would ride hard and take little rest tonight.

Abu Bakr, knowing his children feared for his life, held them both in a long embrace. "*Insha'Allah,*" he said. "If God wills it, we will avoid capture." Reluctantly, Abu Bakr let them go. His family planned to join him in Yathrib soon. The three men mounted their camels to head farther south and then west to the Red Sea. There, far from Mecca's eyes, they would turn northward.

Freedom

By the fourth day of their journey, they had yet to encounter enemies. Abu Bakr, always concerned about the Prophet's safety, chose to be last in line. From this vantage point, he felt he could both keep a watch on Muhammad and survey the undulating horizon of dunes and *wadis*, dry river beds. Behind the others, Abu Bakr also found it quiet enough to pick up distant sounds.

During the hottest hours of the day, the men dismounted, reined the camels into a lying position, and rested against their bodies to avoid the scorching rays of sun. Muhammad, Abu Bakr noted, looked perfectly serene in Qaswa's shade. He slept briefly but deeply, his faith in Allah for the success of their mission unshakable.

They traveled when the heat relented and through much of the night. Darkness also provided cover from the Quraysh. Mostly the men kept quiet, looking for signs of danger, listening to the wool saddlebags swing back and forth with the camels' long strides. The new moon appeared as they neared the Red Sea at dusk. Muhammad looked up at its wisp of silvered light and said, "O crescent of good and of guidance, my faith is in Him who created you!"

When dawn lit the next day, Muhammad and Abu Bakr felt hopeful: They would finally turn north toward their new home. However, soon after they mounted, their excitement disappeared. At first, the dark specks on the horizon looked like rocks, but in a short time, they could see that a small caravan headed straight toward them. Without boulders or trees in the open desert, where could they hide? Already it was too late: If they could see the caravan, the caravan could see them. The three men decided to press on and soon discovered that the man now waving heartily at them, the man leading the caravan, was Abu Bakr's cousin Talhah.

On a return trip from Syria with a load of goods, Talhah had just passed through Yathrib. His group reported that the people there eagerly awaited the Prophet Muhammad's ﷺ arrival at any moment. In fact, a group of Companions and Helpers kept a vigil at the first oasis, the village of Quba, in hopes of seeing Muhammad first.

Talhah looked at the weary travelers and shook his head. He understood the significance of their leaving Mecca, of making a new home where the Believers could worship freely. But the two were dirty and disheveled from hiding. They should not enter their new city in filthy travel robes. They must arrive in the costume of religious pilgrims:

white robes. He presented Muhammad and Abu Bakr with new garments of Syrian cloth for the entry.

On September 27, 622 CE, Muhammad, Abu Bakr, and their guide rode their camels up the last slope of the hills surrounding Quba. The black rocks doubled the sun's heat. Most travelers would wait until dusk to climb this mountain, but they persevered through the hottest part of the day. In Quba, they would finally be safe.

When Muhammad reached the summit and looked ahead, he saw the land precisely as it was in his dream: "the well-watered land between two tracts of black stones." Lush date palms and orchards filled the space between two lava flows. Muhammad took a deep breath. He had not seen this valley since spending time here as a toddler, his memory of those days clouded by his mother's death on the return to Mecca.

No one expected them at this mid-day hour, and all but one person had returned home from the morning vigil. When he saw Muhammad and Abu Bakr's white garments gleaming against the black scree slope, he shouted the alarm: "He is come! He is come!"

By the time Muhammad and Abu Bakr set foot in the oasis, Companions, Believers, Helpers, and villagers crowded into the farthest palm grove to welcome them.

"*As-salaam alaykum!* Peace be upon you!" Muhammad said with a wide smile, ducking underneath a wayward cluster of dates.

"Wa alaykum as-salaam!" they replied in unison. "And peace be upon you!"

Muhammad halted Qaswa. He looked from face to face, his warmth and gratitude for their sacrifices evident in his gaze. For the first time, they would all have freedom to worship. "Spread peace," he said, his arm sweeping the horizon. "Feed the hungry, honor kinship ties, pray while others sleep, and you shall enter paradise."

Muhammad rested three nights in Quba, laying the foundation for a mosque, a place of worship. He stayed with a man of the Aws tribe, and Abu Bakr stayed with a family from the Khazraj. Ali, Muhammad's dear cousin, had fled Mecca after the Prophet's nighttime escape and now joined them.

Word soon reached Muhammad that the people of Yathrib were anxious for his arrival, so the next day, they began the formal procession into the city. Because they had sworn to protect him, the Khazraj tribe's armed guards flanked Muhammad on one side while guards of the Aws lined the other side. Crowds gathered along the roadside— Muhammad's first Companions, the Believers from Mecca, the Helpers who had welcomed the immigrants into their homes, and the curious who wanted to see the Prophet for themselves. "Come is the Prophet of God! Come is the Prophet of God!" they shouted.

Each person wanted the honor of being his host, pleading, "Stay with me, O Messenger of God, for we have strength and protection and abundant food for you!"

Muhammad spoke to this kindness. He blessed the Helpers for sharing their food and homes with the newly arrived Believers. But when they reached out to stay Qaswa's halter, he said, "Let her go her way, for she is under the command of God."

Muhammad lifted Qaswa's reins so that she understood he wanted her to move, then he asked the crowd to let the camel walk freely, for she would decide where to build the first *masjid*, or mosque, in Yathrib. They backed away so that Qaswa could move wherever Allah led her.

Qawsa headed toward the exact place where Muhammad had spent time as a child. Muhammad's kinsmen begged him to stay, yet Muhammad told them the same thing he had said to the others: "Let Qaswa go her way, for she is under God's command." The camel continued on toward a courtyard belonging to two of the first converts in Yathrib—two of the men who had met Muhammad outside the hills of Mecca and pledged their support, As'ad and Awf.

The camel entered the courtyard, which was in a state of ruin, and headed for a small prayer niche As'ad had set up since his conversion. Muhammad let go of her reins. Qaswa walked over to the niche, knelt on her forelegs, then soon rose and walked back toward the entrance. Then she stopped, circled back to the prayer niche, and knelt again. When she flattened her chest against the ground, Muhammad knew he'd found the place of his new home and the first mosque. "This, God willing, is the dwelling," Muhammad said and offered to purchase the land. He twisted in his saddle to admire the view from all angles. A date grove climbed a nearby hill like a fat green ribbon. An orchard laden with lemons looked lit from below. A breeze carried the scent of acacia tree blooms. It reminded Muhammad that all the earth is a mosque, a *masjid*—a place of worship.

On this day, the city of Yathrib was re-named Medina, meaning "City of the Prophet." In humble thanks, Muhammad praised God, and then rested his head on his camel's strong neck with a sigh of relief. This day would begin the Islamic calendar—day one, year one—the day the community of Believers, the *ummah*, could at last worship God freely, as the Angel Gabriel had instructed them.

Epilogue

Soon after the flight from Mecca, Muhammad established all five pillars of Islam: declaration of Allah's divine guidance, ritualized prayer five times a day, fasting, charity to the poor, and a pilgrimage to Mecca. For a devout Believer, all areas of life are infused with spiritual effort and discipline.

Replacing diverse tribal laws as well as religious traditions, Islam became the path of spiritual, social, and political reform across Arabia—and eventually well beyond its borders. Muhammad strove to change the social inequalities he observed and suffered in his childhood, always advocating for orphans, widows, women, and the poor. Education of the mind and spirit was key—he encouraged all Believers to learn to read and write, as well as to recite the Quran.

After his move to Medina, Muhammad led the community of Believers until his death, ten years later. For the *ummah* to survive during that time, Muhammad not only wore the mantle of a spiritual teacher and social reformer but also that of a politician. Despite the fact that he married a number of times after his wife of twenty-five years, Khadija, died, all his children but two daughters, Fatima and Zaynab, died before him.

The Quraysh saw the Prophet Muhammad's ﷺ increasing influence in Medina and Arabia as a constant threat and thus waged three wars against him. In the end, Muhammad and many thousands of Believers returned to Mecca peacefully, unarmed, as religious pilgrims robed in white. When Muhammad reclaimed the Kaaba for the God of Abraham, he destroyed the last of the tribal idols within it.

Author's Note

The Prophet Muhammad ﷺ is a remote figure in history, yet his continued influence on humanity means he is not so distant after all. I wrote *Muhammad: The Story of a Prophet and Reformer* because there are few books that place us in Muhammad's time, help us feel both the beauty and perils of desert life, or give us a sense of the tribal traditions that his Prophethood overturned. What was his life like as a child, as a teen, and beyond? How did being orphaned a number of times shape his world? Who and what helped to form his good character? As a son of the desert, did he always bend toward quiet reflection? How did these conditions ready him for the events that earned him the title, Rasul Allah, Messenger of God?

Muhammad Ibn Abdullah received his first revelations at the age of forty. Before that time, little is recorded of his exact words, but the outlines of his youth as an orphan and shepherd are well known. From his late teen years onward,

Muhammad's leadership abilities and good character were lauded throughout Mecca. We also know many details of his days as a merchant, husband, and father. That Muhammad had a deep spiritual life long before the revelations is also clear: He often went to a cave near Mecca for solitary contemplation, and yearly, he stayed there during the month of Ramadan.

After the revelations began, all that Muhammad said and did became important. He was viewed not as divine but as a man divinely led. The words he spoke as a Messenger of God were written down immediately and compiled in the Quran, the holy book of Islam. I've used a number of excerpts from it.

In addition to the revelations recorded in the Quran, Muhammad's wisdom, evidenced in his own words and actions, won him many converts. For many years after his death, his followers collected and worked to verify them—they are called hadith and are considered indispensable teachings as well as models of behavior. The hadith used in this book have been examined and compiled by Muslim biographers of later centuries so that they reflect, as closely as possible, Muhammad's words and actions. The earliest biographies of the Prophet Muhammad ﷺ, which I have also used extensively, were not scrutinized to the same degree as the hadith but are believed to be fairly accurate. Never have I put words in the mouth of the Prophet Muhammad ﷺ that were not recorded in the Quran, in a classical biography, or in a hadith. Nothing is ever spoken by Muhammad in this book that is not taken from traditional sources and believed to be his own words.

In order to give readers a sense of Muhammad's humanity, of the boy and then the man who lived during the sixth and seventh centuries CE, I have enhanced the bare stories from the classical biographies. I used a sensory palette evoking the Arabian Peninsula of long ago for setting scenes, and from my own research and imagination, I added cameos by his kin, tribe, and others who interacted with him. In a few places I have fabricated what others say, but never the quotations from the Prophet himself. Some small scenes not recorded in any hadith have also been added to convey information in a narrative. I have noted these additions, chapter by chapter, at the end of this book.

Everything Muhammad revealed to others reinforced faith in a single God—the same God worshipped by the other Abrahamic religions, Judaism and Christianity. Although today most people employ the words *Islam* and *Muslim* to mean a specific religion and a person who follows it, in the Quran *islam* means not so much a system of beliefs but a private act of faith in One God.

His teachings would force radical changes in tribal society and allegiances, changes that the rich and powerful did not welcome. They tried everything possible—including assassination attempts and war—to make him stop preaching. This book ends at the Hijrah, when the community of Believers was forced to flee Mecca and move to Yathrib. Afterward, Yathrib would forever be called Medina—the City of the Prophet. Muslims mark the joyous hour when Muhammad entered Medina as the start of the Islamic calendar. This date signals the solemn moment when they could finally worship freely and without fear.

Background Information and Resources

Muhammad's Timeline

570	Birth, orphaned by father
575	Orphaned by mother
578	Grandfather dies and uncle becomes guardian
580–594	Teen years: works as a shepherd, trains as a merchant
595	Weds Khadija
610	First revelation
613	Makes revelations public
615	Persecution of Muhammad's followers by the Quraysh
617	Boycott of the Banu Hashim and Muhammad
619 or 620	Year of Sorrow
622	Muhammad's followers emigrate to Yathrib, thereafter called Medina
625–628	Military period
630	Peaceful conquest of Mecca
632	Death

Glossary of Arabic Terms

Allah: the Arabic word for God (*al* means "the," and *ilah* means "sole deity")

Ansar: the Helpers, members of Yathrib's tribes who joined Muhammad's community of Believers.

Hadith: sayings and actions attributed to the Prophet; collected over the century or so after Muhammad's death, biographers evaluate their authenticity based on the reliability of their transmission through chains of narrators

Hijrah: the emigration of Muhammad's followers from Mecca to Yathrib due to persecution from the Quraysh

Islam: In the historical context of the Quran, *islam* was a noun denoting a personal act of submission to God—the God of all three Abrahamic faiths. In time, as Muhammad's followers needed to differentiate themselves from other communities, *islam* became a noun denoting a religion. As there are no capitals or lowercase letters in Arabic, Islam (with the letter i capitalized) is now the norm in translation.

Kaaba: the ancient sanctuary believed to have been built by either Adam or the Prophet Abraham and his son Isaac

Mosque or Masjid: a fixed, communal place of prayer; however, since God is everywhere, a Believer can use a prayer carpet as a portable place of prayer

Muslim: in modern usage, an adjective or noun describing a follower of Islam. For Muhammad and his followers, Jews and Christians who submitted fully to God were also called *muslim*. The Prophets Abraham and Moses, as well as Jesus, are declared *muslim* in the Quran. The use of the word *Muslim* with the m capitalized was a convention bestowed by European academics on the followers of Islam because they wanted to differentiate between religious groups and practices.

Quraysh: the tribe that inhabited and ruled Mecca in pre-Islamic Arabia

Quran: the holy book, the central text, of Islam, which Muslims believe to be the revealed word of God given to Muhammad over approximately twenty-three years through the Angel Gabriel

Rasul Allah: Messenger of God

Ummah: the community of Believers who followed the Prophet Muhammad ﷺ

The Five Pillars of Islam

Shahadah: the Muslim profession of faith: "There is no god but God, and Muhammad is God's Messenger"

Salat: the required five daily prayers for Muslims—just before sunrise, just after noon, mid-afternoon, after sunset, and evening

Sawm: religious fasting, as in the annual, month-long fast for Muslims called Ramadan, during which Muslims do not eat or drink during daylight hours

Zakat: mandatory alms given to the poor

Hajj: an annual pilgrimage to Mecca that is required of every able-bodied Muslim who can afford to do so at least once in a lifetime

Sources

Biographies

Armstrong, Karen. *Muhammad: A Prophet for Our Time*. New York: HarperCollins, 2007.

Aslan, Reza. *No god but God: The Origins, Evolution and Future of Islam*. New York: Random House, 2007.

Lings, Martin. *Muhammad: His Life Based on the Earliest Sources*. Rochester, Vermont: Inner Traditions, 2006.

Newby, Gordon D. *A Concise Encyclopedia of Islam*. Oxford: Oneworld, 2002.

Ramadan, Tariq. *In the Footsteps of the Prophet: Lessons from the Life of Muhammad*. Oxford: Oxford University Press, 2007.

Quran

Royal Aal al-Bayt Institute translation, Altafasir.com

Chapter Notes

The Orphan It is well known that Aminah, Muhammad's mother, sought out a wet nurse for him among the Bedouins and that Barakah was Muhammad's servant for the duration of her lifetime. As with every chapter, sensory and scene details have been added.

The Shepherd Halimah's story and her words are reported in the early biographies. While the general facts of Bedouin life at this time are known, this specific story of Muhammad is not mentioned in any biography; the scene is based on inference from what is known of his life as a young shepherd.

City of Gods This scene is created to convey the known facts and outlines of Muhammad's life with his grandfather.

Signs This story of Muhammad's encounter with the monk Bahirah, including the dialogue, is well known and documented in early biographies.

Al-Amin: The Trustworthy Khadija's hiring of Muhammad to supervise a trading mission and the words of the subsequent marriage proposal through her go-between are well noted in the earliest biographies. Only the sensory and scene details are added.

At the Center of the World The rebuilding of the Kaaba and Muhammad's role and words as a mediator are well established in the early biographies of him.

Home This entire scene was created to convey, in a narrative, a number of known facts about Muhammad and Khadija's life. The specific story is not in any biography.

The Angel The words spoken in this first encounter between the Angel Gabriel and Muhammad are the central event in the Prophet Muhammad's ﷺ life and are well documented in biographies and in the Quran (Q96:1–5). I added "Read" after the command "Recite!" to the translation of the Angel's first command to Muhammad. Although illiterate, Muhammad, like most peoples of desert tribal culture, was skilled in recitation and memorization, a fact stressed in this book several times. So when Muhammad replies to the angel that he is incapable of doing what the angel asks, I leaned on Tariq Ramadan's translation of the angel's first command: "Read!" in his book *In the Foosteps of the Prophet: Lessons from the Life of Muhammad*. What ensues with Khadija and her relative, Waraqah, is well established.

Companions This scene was created to convey information about the fledgling community of Companions and how they worshipped. All the verses cited are from the Quran (Q30:20–24).

Not for the Sun The first scene of Muhammad preaching typifies the situation that led to Muhammad's confrontations with the Quraysh. It is not in any biography, but Muhammad's words are from hadith and the Quran (Q112:1–4 and Q1:2–7). The words and actions in the scene in which the Quraysh nobles confront Abu Talib are well known through biographies as are the words Abu Talib says later to Muhammad.

Raise the Dead! The story of Bilal is recorded in the early biographies. The scene in which Muhammad learns about Bilal's fate is imagined. In the scene outside the Kaaba, the harassment Muhammad suffered and the words spoken to him by the Quraysh are well documented by Muhammad's biographers.

The Refusal This story is well known in the trusted biographies of Muhammad. The verse Muhammad recited from the Quran is Q41:37. The sensory details of the scene were added.

The First to Flight The story of the Companions winning the protection of the Christian King in Abyssinia is well reported by the early biographers. Ja'far quotes from the Quran (Q19: 20–21).

The Boycott The proclamation boycotting the Hashimites is well documented. The sensory details of the scene were added.

The Prophet of Arabia This scene was created to summarize the effect of the Quraysh ban. The words Muhammad speaks are from hadith and the Quran (Q94: 6, Q2: 257).

The End of the Ban The ending of the Quraysh boycott at the Kaaba is a well-documented story; only sensory details have been added.

Year of Sorrow This scene was created to describe the long-term effects of the Companions' persecution. The words spoken by Muhammad are from hadith.

The Vision The three anecdotes told in this chapter are well-reported incidents in Muhammad's life. Sensory details have been added.

Insha'Allah The words spoken between Muhammad and the men of Yathrib are well documented; sensory detail, as well as some verses from the Quran (Q20: 53–54), have been added.

The Helpers   The oath made to Muhammad by the leaders of the Aws and Khazraj peoples is well documented; sensory details were added to create the scene.

Flight   This event is well documented in biographies.

The Assassins   The assassination attempt described in this chapter is well established. The verse Muhammad recites from the Quran is Q41:37. The sensory details of the scene were added.

The Cave   Muhammad's faith in God—when Muhammad is saved by the appearance of a dove and spider—makes this story one of the most beloved in his biographies. The description of the scene was added.

Freedom   The events during the journey to freedom are well known from early biographies, as is Muhammad's founding of the first mosque in Yathrib. The sensory description of the scene was added.